C000279838

LANDMARK COLLECTOR'S LIBRARY

THE SPIRIT OF LEEK: 2

THE 20TH CENTURY IN PHOTOGRAPHS

Cathryn Walton & Lindsey Porter

LANDMARK COLLECTOR'S LIBRARY

THE SPIRIT OF
L E E K : 2
THE 20TH CENTURY IN PHOTOGRAPHS

Cathryn Walton & Lindsey Porter

Landmark Publishing

Published by

Ashbourne Hall, Cokayne Ave
Ashbourne, Derbyshire DE6 1EJ England
Tel: (01335) 347349 Fax: (01335) 347303
e-mail: landmark@clara.net
web site: www.landmarkpublishing.co.uk

1st edition

ISBN 1 84306 009 4

© **Cathryn Walton & Lindsey Porter 2001**

The rights of Cathryn Walton & Lindsey Porter as authors of this work
has been asserted by them in accordance with the Copyright,
Design and Patents Act, 1993.

All rights reserved. No part of this publication may be reproduced,
stored in a retrieval system or transmitted in any form or by any means,
electronic, mechanical, photocopying, recording or otherwise without
the prior permission of Landmark Publishing Ltd.

British Library Cataloguing in Publication Data: a catalogue
record for this book is available from the British Library.

Printed by MPG Ltd, Bodmin, Cornwall

Design & reproduction by able design

Cover by James Allsopp

Front cover: Ball Haye Road at Park Vale
Back cover:
Top: A cheapjack, Derby Street   **Middle** 4th Leek Scouts Club Day   **Bottom** Mill Street
Page 1: High Street with the Grand Cinema as originally built
Page 2 upper: Highfield Hall, home of the Nicholsons; **lower:** Leek Cyclist Club outside the Duke of
York Inn in Derby Street
Title page: Old Chris, the road sweeper, whose cheerful face was a familiar sight in Leek streets in the
1960s

Contents

Introduction

Since the publication of Volume 1 last year, we have been heartened by the considerable interest we received for our book. We had intended to complete our work with this volume. However, we could have included much more on the themes covered in these pages and we still haven't covered the textile industry – the many mills which exist, or used to exist – within the streets of the town.

We therefore hope to produce a Volume 3 next year covering all the town's textile mills and associated factories, such as dyeworks. If you have any photographs covering such places, or even social events of the workers, photographs of factory activities of all descriptions, we would like to see them. Please contact Cath Walton on 01538 388429 or Lindsey Porter at Ashbourne on 01335 347349. We would love to hear from you.

We have brought together in this book many photographs of streets not covered in Volume 1, plus scenes of the canal and railway; in our schools; at Blackshaw Moor's Polish Community; scenes of people at work; the town at war; and what we expect to be a popular section – pubs around the town! Then there are people enjoying themselves – we could have included many more here if we had had more space.

Our selection, we hope, will bring back memories for many people. Above all, we hope it helps to create a fitting record of life in Leek in the 20th century.

Many thanks to all who have helped to put this volume together. These include:

Ken Bowyer, the late Arthur Goldstraw who took many of the street scenes, Yvonne Goldstraw, Jo Greenwood, Graham Grindey, Eileen Hall, Margaret Hall, Fred & Val Holland, Marian Hulme, Christine Hunt, Basil Jeuda (Gordon Walwyn Collection), the late George Keats, Susan Keates, Leek & District Historical Society, Leek& Moorlands Historical Trust, Leek Post & Times, Rowena Lovatt, Harold Mace, the late Janet McKeith, Gerald Mee, George Oultram, DK Pedley, Ray Poole, David Rhead, Mrs Salmons, Ann Sharratt, Ralph Sharratt, Brian Simpson, Staffordshire County Council: Local History Collection at Leek Library, Peggy Starling, J Stubbs, Stasia Tomlinson, Brian & Kathleen Turner; George Walton, Norman Wright.

If we have missed someone, please forgive us and tell us – we will make amends in Volume 3.

We recognise that it is impossible to determine who took some of the images we have collected but we have tried to obtain permission wherever we believed it was necessary. If we have missed someone, we offer our apologies. We have deliberately not used some photographs where we could not clear copyright.

Cathryn Walton and Lindsey Porter 2001

In the days of the stage coach Ashbourne Road was known as the London Road. Travellers leaving Leek would pass through wild moorland country over Leek Moor before heading towards Derby. It was renamed Ashbourne Road at the beginning of the 20 th century.

Nowadays Ashbourne Road has relatively few shops but in the first half of the 20th century it boasted an impressive range of them, milliners, tailors, shoemakers, butchers, blacksmiths, grocers, newsagents, fried fish dealers and hairdressers all plied their trade here.

One of the Straker steam buses which operated between Leek, Waterhouses and Hulme End. They provided a link to the narrow gauge railway line at Waterhouses. These vehicles were purchased from Straker and Co in 1904 at a cost of £700 each when the light railway opened. They were chain driven, coke fired and weighed over two tons unladen. Their solid tyres made for an uncomfortable ride and passengers who endured their jolting journeys nicknamed them "Earthquake 1& 2". Behind the bus can be seen Sparrow Park and the old public baths. On the extreme right is Goldstraw's Salt Warehouse.

The Straker Steam bus loading passengers outside the Talbot. Of equal interest are the houses on the right which were situated in front of Smithfield Terrace.

The Coffee Tavern with Smithfield Cottages to the rear. Opened in 1878 (see Volume 1), The Coffee Tavern was supported by the Temperance Society to encourage the working classes to abstain from alcohol. It provided a venue where people could eat without the opportunity to purchase alcoholic beverages! In later years the Smithfield Commercial Restaurant operated from these premises. Many people will remember the Sharpe family who ran this establishment.

The rear of the building with a stairwell attached. The houses shown on p7 behind the steam bus occupied the open area behind. Smithfield Terrace is on the left.

A sad day – the demolition of yet another part of Leek's history as The Coffee Tavern is pulled down.

A scene of desolation as The Coffee Tavern is demolished. The Talbot Hotel still stands but the chimney of Brough, Nicholson and Hall has long since disappeared.

Another view of the cottages between the White Lion Inn and The Coffee Tavern. These cottages were situated on what was once known as Alsop's Bank. The photograph was taken during the 1897 Jubilee Celebrations.

Houses which made up Smithfield Terrace. The new Cattle Market or Smithfield in Haywood Street gave it's name to this row of houses. On the1881 census they are enumerated as 1 to 8 Alsop's Row although there appears to be only seven houses. Mr Alsop had a factory in the building which later became The Coffee Tavern.

A view from the Cattle Market looking towards The Coffee Tavern and the rear of the houses which later became known as Smithfield Terrace.

Here we can see the two-storey building once owned by Beech, the builders, which was Leeks last smithy. The large building was a nicely proportioned textile mill. The three-storey house beyond the smithy has been demolished. It also had a frontage to Cross Street. Peeping out at the end of the properties are the petrol pumps of Hodkinson's Filling station which tragically caught fire in 1969.

Opened in 1880 at 30, London Road, this branch of the Leek and Moorlands Industrial Provident Society Ltd., also provided a bakery. The Society later reverted to it's original name of the Leek and Moorlands Co-operative Society. New central premises designed by Larner Sugden were built here in 1899 as the plaque on the building confirms. The lovely terracotta and cream friezes, bearing the words: "Building; gardening; weaving; Leek Half; mechanic; farming and trade", have recently been restored. Refurbished in 1997, by the Staffordshire Housing Association after falling into disrepair, the building contains 7 flats and has been renamed Penny Bank House.

Looking towards Ashbourne Road from Moorhouse Street with the weaver's cottages in the background which were adjacent to the old smithy.

A close up of the smithy at 19 & 21, Ashbourne Road. John James Meakin worked as a blacksmith and wheelwright here for many years.

A delightful photograph looking towards the smithy along Moorhouse Street, a reminder of the fact that this area was formerly part of Moor House Farm. Many years ago this land was owned by a member of the Grosvenor family, hence the name Grosvenor Street which is off to the right.

Hodkinson's Filling Station where the petrol pumps were on the edge of the pavement. In August 1969 petrol vapours were ignited by a naked flame on a gas powered refrigerator inside the building. The resulting conflagration ignited the cab of a petrol tanker parked outside on the road. As the intense heat began to blister the paint on the tanker Arthur Allen, a leading fireman, climbed inside the cab of the tanker and released the brake. The tanker was in imminent danger of exploding and at the time burning petrol was running down the street. Mr Hodkinson, who had been pulled from the building by his son David, later died as a result of his injuries. Both Mr Allen and David showed incredible bravery that day.

These cottages were behind Hodkinson's filling station. The rear of these houses may be seen in the next photograph, to the left of the telegraph pole.

Cross Street, looking towards Ashbourne Road. The building on the right was part of Brough, Nicholson and Hall's mill. It was single-storey at street level and had a slate roof.

Next to the three-storey house in the above photograph was this property with two dwellings shoehorned in on a tiny plot.

A reminder that the Ashbourne Road led to a rural area as sheep are driven to their new homes after leaving the Cattle Market. Life seemed to have a slower pace, children had time to stand and stare, while a trap loaded with baskets makes its leisurely way along the road.

A sweeping view down Ashbourne Road with its elegant Victorian houses. Further down on the right are York Mill and London Mill, both part of the Brough, Nicholson and Hall complex.

A solitary cart wends its way up the road and out of town. Wardle Sales' dyehouse (now Charles Leek & Sons Ltd) and Springfield Road do not exist, or the housing development which now stretches to the hospital.

These houses stood between Ashbourne Road and Prospect Road. Traditionally known as The Old Barracks, they comprised blocks of 2,4 and 6 houses around a communal yard. Only one house had a toilet at the bottom of the garden; all the other toilets stood in a row along one side of the yard. Long gardens stretched away from each house. The occupants were moved to Windsor Drive and Springfield Road in 1959 while the Barracks were demolished. On 3rd January 1961, Mrs Eileen Hall moved into her house in Prospect Road. All the former residents of the Barracks were offered accommodation in the new houses near to their former homes.

The last occupant of this house, a Mrs Traynor, stated that a dress length for Queen Mary was woven in the attic. It is true that many houses in the town had long attics called shades where weaving took place. Some of these houses can still be seen in King Street and London Street. This view looks towards the Flying Horse. The Moorlands Hospital is visible on the extreme left. This building was formerly Leek's Union Workhouse which opened in 1839. Messrs Bateman and Drury of Birmingham designed the workhouse in a classical style. An infirmary block opened in1898 designed by J T Brearly, the Leek architect.

Above: The old, stone arched Lowe Hill Bridge was built in 1828 to carry the lane from Knivedon to Lowe Hill. The arch was dynamited after the removal of two tablets giving its date of construction. These stone tablets were then built into the new bridge.

Left: Pickwood Hall, home for many years of William Challinor a member of the Challinor family of lawyers who practised in Leek. The firm of Challinor and Shaw at 10, Derby Street will be well known to many readers. In 1887, William Challinor gave some of his land to the town to create Pickwood Recreation Ground.

This photograph shows the scene on Sunday morning following the demolition of the bridge during the night.

When the new bridge was constructed ten pre-cast concrete beams, each weighing over five tons, were put into place using a specialist crane. This new bridge, constructed in 1961, is over 35 feet wide, nearly twice as wide as the old one. Officially opened by Councillor TS Barlow in January 1961 the new Lowe Hill bridge cost £20,000.

One of the Straker buses returning from Waterhouses. Drivers of horse drawn vehicles would dismount to hold the bridle of their horses, as there was a danger that the horse would bolt as the noisy steam bus approached. These buses were limited to eight miles an hour, but even so the passengers experienced a rather rough ride. During the time of their service in Leek a claim was made against them for damage to road surfaces. Unfortunately one driver was drawn over the coals when the steam bus gave an unexpected lurch and the days taking's, from the light railway at Waterhouses, vanished into the fire box instead of being safely transported to Leek.

Early day trippers! An outing from Leek stops at Lowe Hill for a photograph.

These proud poplar trees stood at the top of Ashbourne Road and gave their name to Poplar Garage, run by Vin and Margaret Smith. Behind the trees on the right was the brickyard of Thomas Porter and Son. The lock-up garages behind the terraced houses are sited on the infilled marl pit. The company also had brickworks at Brown Edge and Cellarhead and there were other brick pits on Ashbourne Road. The fire station in Springfield Road was built on one of them in 1967.

Below left: Poplar Garage in the 1960s. Note the demolition of the houses in the background. Above: the garage following redevelopment and below: the arrival of a new fuel tank. The fuel price shows the price of petrol some twenty or so years ago.

These houses stood at the corner of Buxton Road and Ball Haye Road, those facing the camera having been empty for years. The site is now occupied by the Park Medical Centre.

To the left of the above view (and adjoining the left hand house) was this roofless property. To the left of this was the burnt out Victoria Mill adjacent to the Park Inn. This will feature in Volume 3. Notice the old fashioned road sign.

These houses on the Buxton Road between Brunswick and Portland Street have all been demolished. Only the three houses on the left, just past Brunswick Street still stand. There appears to be little wrong with these properties and strikes one as being a waste of potentially good housing stock. In 1881 the houses were numbered from 72 to 94 Buxton Road and occupied by a variety of people who mainly worked in the silk industry. Charles Cope, a clock cleaner, lived at number 96 and James Whitehouse, a cooper resided at number 90. The house nearest the camera was obviously a shop and in 1881 was kept by William Harvey who was a carver, gilder and grocer! In later years Charles Kirkham, a general printer, occupied this property.

Houses in Portland Street which were all demolished under a clearance scheme. The factory and its foreshortened chimney still survive. The former housing site is now used by A J Worthington Ltd.

These houses on the corner of Weston Street were built by 1856 and demolished just over a hundred years later in September 1960. These three houses were back to back with two houses and a shop. Weston Street took its name from the owner of the land on which the houses were built.

These seven properties fronted Buxton Road and were adjacent to the houses in the previous photograph. Leek Day Nursery and Leek Day Centre now stand on this site.

This branch of the Leek and Moorlands Co-operative Society Ltd stood at the corner of Osbourne Street and Buxton Road. The shop occupied this premises at 108, Buxton Road from the early 20th century. This multi-purpose shop was not only a grocers, confectioners, drapers and tailors, but also a boot and shoe dealer and coal merchant! Note the advertisement for Pelaw cake flour on the window.

In 1870 Fred Adams bought a small dairy farm from the Earl of Macclesfield, on Buxton Road. His son, also Fred, started butter making here in 1922. This business became the first in the country to produce pre-packed butter. Adams Dairies became Adams Butter Ltd and then Adams Food Ltd. By 1975 it was the largest organisation in the country selling butter. The Springfield Road site, which took its name from the original Springfield Farm (shown here), was advertised for sale in the Leek Post and Times in 1990.

TELEPHONE 215

BOOK AT Mr. J. Sherratt, St. Edward Street, Leek ;
Mr. Ben Tatton, Ball Haye Green ; or main office.

Harold Hall

CHARABANC . PROPRIETOR

Old Royal Oak Garage,
BUXTON ROAD,
LEEK, Staffs.

Pleasure Excursions arranged any
distance.

THE "MOORLAND QUEEN"

WILL RUN AS FOLLOWS :

DATE	DESTINATION	START AT	FARE

Mr Harold Hall ran a charabanc service from the Royal Oak Garage in Buxton Road. The charabanc was known as the Moorland Queen and is pictured here at the Waste. Mr Hall ran trips to Dovedale, the Cat and Fiddle, Hulme End, Derby and Shuttlingslow. You could travel to the Wrekin, Boscobel for 13s 6d and could order "luncheon, tea and drinkables" for an extra 2s 6d to 5s. These prices were applicable in 1910!

The Moorland Queen was a duel service vehicle, each November the body of the vehicle was changed, a long body being added in winter. Thus the vehicle was able to be used to carry corn, coal and ashes during the winter months.

Right: an advert for the Royal Oak Garage for July 1941. At this time it was being run by Mr Emberton.

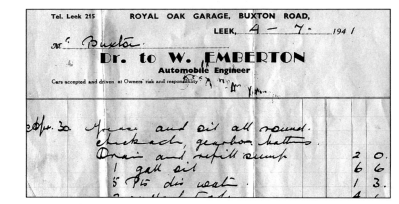

Below: another group of people about to depart Leek Market Place on another charabanc trip.

One of Adams Butter lorries fast in snow (believed to be Buxton Road)

An old view of Ball Haye Green. Shown empty of traffic here, it is now a main feeder road to the Haregate housing estate. How different our streets would look without the curse of parked cars.

Another unusual, but well known vehicle, was Mr Bestwick's coal-fired steam car! It was painted blue and it was said that its whistle was from the Flying Dutchman loco. It certainly made an impression when it was used on the streets. We understand it was built by Mr Bestwick and sold after his death. Here are two views of the car – in Brough Park and outside his shop in Ball Haye Street.

Fountain Street festooned with bunting to celebrate a royal visit. Cawdry Buildings are to the right and the Fountain Street Chapel is to the left.

This elegant house at 1, Queen Street was once the home of Robert Wright, a silk manufacturer. It is now the shop and workshop of Smith, Bainbridge & Wardle.

Reg Talbot's greengrocers shop at 10, Cawdry Buildings in Fountain Street. In the early years of the 20th century, this was a drapers shop kept by Charles and Sarah Ward. By 1932 it had become Harold Bell's Pharmacy. Cawdry Buildings were built in the grounds of Cawdry House which features on page 93 of Volume 1.

Left: This property adjacent to the Fountain Inn in Fountain Street was demolished to make way for Leek's new Police Station. The Fountain is another of Leek's old inns having been established on this site from at least 1837. Fountain Street probably stands on the site of an old medieval road; the present street takes its name from the reservoir, dating from the 18th century. This used to be at the eastern end of the street bounded also by The Organ Ground and East Street. A new housing estate now stands on the site of this old reservoir.

Head out of town towards the Macclesfield Road and you will travel down Mill Street. It is almost unrecognisable from the busy, bustling, close-knit community pictured here. Nearly all of the old houses have been demolished leaving just a few isolated properties which still survive. The people who lived and worked here stuck together through thick and thin, supporting each other in bad times and celebrating together on joyful occasions. Mill Street was a community all on its own.

Gas lamps, gables and garretts huddle together as rainwater glistens from the cobbles in this evocative picture of old Mill Street. Originally the name of Mill Street was only given to that part of the road by the corn mill. The steeper top part was known in the late 17th century as 'the Hollow Lane' before it was cut through to make the highway we know today.

All that is left of the 'Royal Oak' which stood at 23, Mill Street. Its hanging sign can be seen on the left of the street in the photograph on page 34. The Fisher family were landlords here for several decades.

Bertie Crosby's grocers shop at 134, Mill Street just across the road from the Ragged School.
The advertisements for tobacco and cigarettes seem incongruous among the temptingly displayed fruit. One commodity is good for your health and the other definitely is not!

On the outside of Biddulph's shop at 33, Mill Street, advertisements for Windolene, Colman's Starch, Park Drive and Woodbines feature prominently. Just below the shop and behind the hoardings is a brick A.R.P. post built during World War II by Turners the builders. The steep steps of Donkey Bank can be seen to the right of this photograph.

Biddulph's shop can be located just below the lamp post in the centre of the photograph. West Street School is visible on the upper left corner. To the right is Wardle & Davenport's mill with its tall chimney. On the extreme right is William Sugden's Big Mill built in 1857 and first occupied by Joseph Broster.

Above: This group of recessed houses adjoined the right hand house in the bottom photograph of the previous page. Out of sight on the left hand side was one of the smallest houses in Leek (see below).

Left: two views of the houses below Donkey Bank steps, dwarfed by Wardle & Davenport's mill. At one time these houses were owned by a farmer named Hidderley who rented them out. The families who lived in them were quite poor sharing one lavatory between three houses. In 1881, the cottages below Donkey Bank steps were inundated with earth when several tons fell into their back yards, damaging doors and windows. The ground had slipped down the bank from an extension to the playground of West Street School; fortunately no one was hurt.

The railings on the pavement mark the start of the Donkey Bank steps. West Street School was affectionately known as 'Donkey Bank College' after this old right of way. Another set of steps on the other side of the street gave access to Nab Hill.

Above: lower down Mill Street stands The Jester, once the Kings Arms public house. The property to the right of the pub is now part of The Jester, but the entry has now gone.

Below: a newsagents shop heads the row of cottages above the Ragged School. The Sugden designed Ragged School and chapel opened in 1871 when 130 children attended (the original Ragged School began in May 1865 in two cottages in Belle Vue). After falling into disrepair over many years this building has now been converted into flats and gained a new lease of life. The railing marking the way up to Belle Vue can be seen between the cottages and the Ragged School. It also features on the top photograph on page 41.

Another view of the cottages between the Kings Arms and the Ragged School. The house on the extreme right has an interesting set of steps leading to the front door, complete with a wooden hand rail. It has a rather delapidated exterior and looks as if it may be boarded up.

Left: Set in the cobble stones near to the parked car (below) were two mill stones from Leek mill. Here is one of them.

Behind these hoardings was Wheatley's yard. It was previously owned by Tom Beech a scrap iron merchant. His merchandise stretched from Mill Street to Kingsway (the local name for Belle Vue Road) and was an endless source of fascination for children making their way to school. In 1919, Tom Beech bought the houses at 111, 113, and 115, Mill Street which he rented. The vendor was the Earl of Macclesfield who sold the houses for £500. In 1904, Ralph Beech was an iron merchant at 115, Mill Street; presumably he was Tom's father. Prior to the Beech family occupying this site it was a joiner's shop and yard run by Noah Tatton. He occupied the premises for several years around the turn of the 20th century.

The large shop front denotes the Leek and Moorlands Co-operative Society shop at 123-127, Mill Street. To the left of the 'Co-op' was Bowcock's fish and chip shop and to the right is the Blue Ball Inn. The 'Co-op' later became Terry Wheatley's chip shop; for some reason he was not allowed to sell fish!

This view completes the properties on the south side of Mill Street. Belle Vue goes up to the right along with Kiln Lane. The house on the corner of Mill Street and Belle Vue was Nellie Wignall's shop. The dye house on the left survives. The three-storey property in the middle of the photograph may be seen on page 50 too.

The remains of this ancient property were revealed in 1963 following the demolition of cottages adjacent to the Dyers Arms. It was built of sandstone and has since disappeared. The building seemed to have a frontage to Kiln Lane and had cellars. Was it a pub prior to the construction of the Dyers Arms and was it one of the oldest properties in Low Hamil to have been built in stone?

The end of Mill Street and the beginning of Kiln Lane. These properties were also victims of the demolition man. The large window in the white property denotes Edward Barker's confectioners shop at 175, Mill Street.

Looking up Kiln Lane we can see one of Leek's 'double houses'. The property at the bottom of the four-storey building was entered at the front in Kiln Lane while the property at the top was approached from the back in Belle Vue. Two houses in one!

The following pages cover the properties on the north side of the street. The fascinating photograph above dates from the late 1950s. The Royal Oak Inn survives on the left although properties higher up have already been demolished. The properties on the right are shown intact as far as the bend. Nearest the camera was a workshop and then came the tallest and smallest houses in the town. The tall building was a double house, two houses on top of each other, one with its entrance in Mill Street and the other with its entrance in Clerk Bank. Next to this double house was a three-storey building and adjoining that was the smallest house.

The smallest house in Leek in March 1958. It was six inches narrower than 55, Mill Street seen on page 39. It was next to Pedley's, see page 46.

No 22, Mill Street.
In 1872 it was the blacksmiths shop of Charles Henry Bold and was known as Smithy House. Samuel Yates, a marine store dealer, occupied the house in the early 1900s followed by Arthur Pedley a carter. Mr Pedley plied his trade with a horse and cart but when Alfred Pedley took over he used a lorry.

Left: of all the photographs of Mill Street shown in this book, this is the only one showing this group of properties in the middle of the street, portrayed here on a winter's day.

Crosby's grocers shop can be seen in the middle of these properties (see also page 36). These tall houses show evidence of shades on the third floor where silk twisters and weavers once worked.

Trees soften the aspect of working class Mill Street where houses stood shoulder to shoulder, jostling for space. The hanging sign of the Nag's Head can be seen on the left, opposite the former King's Arms. If the locals didn't choose to drink at these establishments they might walk up to the Royal Oak or stroll down to the Blue Ball, the Dyers Arms or the Dog and Rot (the Conservative Club)! The cart on the left may be one of the gas collectors carts. These carts were pushed around by the gas collectors when they emptied the meters; they were always safely padlocked.

The inhabitants of Mill Street Square prepare for the coronation festivities in 1953. Yards of bunting flutter frivolously as it is hung between the houses.

The situation of this property can be identified by the new development taking place behind it. The former Leek Urban District Council built the new property to the rear. This rare scene shows a three-storey house in one of the Courts on the north side of Mill Street.

The bottom of Mill Street showing the Blue Ball on the right and the interesting, varying styles of architecture of the properties to the left. Cottages and houses hold their own against imposing weavers' shades and factory premises. The street sign of Court No 12 can be seen to the left. Mill Street was riddled with courts lined with houses set behind the street. Some kind of celebratory activity appears to be taking place outside the Blue Ball.

The four-storey building seen on the previous photograph is being demolished in this scene. Scaffolding has been erected and two men are perched on the roof. Note the barbers pole above the shop on the left.

The house set back on the far left is one of the few in the street to have survived. The end three-storey property is already boarded up. On the right the entry beneath the white sign gave access to Court No 8. The shop displays signs for Park Drive and Senior Service cigarettes. These buildings may be seen on page 49.

The building (top of page 51) may also be seen on the extreme right of the photograph below. There is a tradition in the town that this was the workshop of James Brindley, the famous millwright, who built the corn mill nearby. His workshop was apparently near the bottom of Mill Street and this was the only building which had an entrance for a cart. Whether it dates from the 18th century, however, is not known. The new building on the extreme right below also features on page 48.

This and adjacent properties were demolished in 1963.

The scene around the Abbey Green Road. The old Spread Eagle still survives as the Conservative Working Men's Club but the chimney of the Hencroft Works and the properties above Abbey Green Road have all disappeared. The building on the far right may also be seen on page 50.

Old houses adjacent to the Conservative Club; the house on the right was once lived in by Mrs Stonier, affectionately known as Old Mother Stonier.

Another view of the houses next to the Conservative Club.

The building demolished on the right of these photographs is reputed to have been the home of the last abbot of Dieulacress, after the dissolution of his abbey.

The same properties seen on the previous page. To the right may be seen the Hencroft Dye Works which has also been demolished.

Mary Clarkson's 'hand', which existed in the paving stone. The inscription reads: 'Mary Clarkson's hand, 1861'.
However, it has not proved possible to locate her in contemporary records. The paving stone was near the bottom of the street, on the north side.

Weavers' Cottages formerly situated near to Bridge End and now demolished.

During the mid 19th century a suburb of mills and houses for the mill workers developed around West Street. These new streets included Albert Street, Angle Street, Westwood Terrace and Picton Street. Building plots were offered for sale in the 1850s on land between Garden Street, Belle Vue and West Street. Pictured here is a row of terraced workers houses in School Street. This street ran up the side of West Street School. This and photographs of adjacent properties were taken in 1964. School Street appears in a sorry state, the houses wait forlornly to be demolished, their windows boarded up and their rooms uninhabited.

Mount Methodist School. Opened in 1815 at a cost of £1,400, this Wesleyan Methodist School developed from a Sunday School. In 1854 the school was rebuilt by Sugden at a cost of £3,000 and in 1855 the mixed day school had 40 pupils who were taught reading, writing and arithmetic. It was extended again in 1881 and by 1885 the school had 458 pupils. Over the years the number of pupils gradually dwindled until there were just 300 pupils in the 1950s and 60s, falling to about 100 after 1981 when its status changed from junior to first school. It was closed in 1983.

The buildings above West Street School (or Donkey Bank College) have been demolished. However, the houses on the extreme right still stand. Many people will remember Loxley's Toffee Shop at 20, West Street and the dress shop just below it. Fashionable young women in the 1960s were able to buy their Mary Quant style dresses at Pandora's.

These houses above the Britannia Inn no longer exist; a car park now occupies this site. The shop on the opposite corner to the Britannia is now Leek Bacon Shop at 48, West Street. This property has changed hands many times over the years, previous traders being Ann Salt, Charles Fernihough, James Brookes (who was a painter and decorator) and George Perry who had a fruit and grocers shop.

Houses in West Street Square. Here the address was Court No 5, West Street. The Square had five houses facing West Street, at one time tenanted by Messrs Leese, Wood, White, Belfield and Plant. The other three houses may be seen overleaf. Leading out of the square were the backs of five houses in Court No 4, West Street, which feature on the lower photograph across. The small building to the left of this photograph was an ashpit. It was used to store ashes from the fire grates in the houses, presumably until they were collected by the ashmen!

Terraced houses in West Street Square. The second house from the right was the home of Old Mother Leese who made ice cream. She kept the ice cream in a large churn and children would call at her house with their basins to be filled with delicious ice cream which was then carefully carried home.

This was taken at the top of Britannia Street with St Stephens Square off to the right. Shown here is the cobbler's shop of Mr Heppinstall; earlier it belonged to a Mr Mottershead. To the left of this shop are the ruins of Stephen Goodwin and Tatton's Britannia Mill. The mill had been destroyed by a fire during World War II, the ruins remaining here and in West Street for many years before being demolished.

Arthur Hay's Cash Supply Stores at 45, West Street. Mr Hay also had another grocers shop at 57, Derby Street (see Spirit of Leek Vol. I, p.100). By 1932 this shop was a high class grocers run by Frederick William Walker. Today, 45, West Street is a wallpaper shop and not long ago was an establishment which sold motor cycles.

Left: one of Walker's invoices from c. 1953.

A set of photographs depicting the opening of Belle Vue Road in 1906. Prior to this date this area was known simply as Belle Vue and before 1841 as Back of the Street. In 1906, Belle Vue was widened so that the street now opened into Mill Street. This provided a route from the bottom of Mill Street to the Railway Station, by passing the town centre. The widening of the road meant that thirteen cottages had to be demolished. Previously the road had only been 10ft wide ending in a passage 4ft in width. The cost of these improvements was £2,370. The road was opened to vehicles on 13 September 1906; the opening ceremony was performed by Sir Thomas Wardle.

The ceremony took place on a very rainy day hence the shower of umbrellas. Some of the cottages shown here on the left hand side of Belle Vue Road (going down) were built up to the sandstone cliff and had no back doors. In the 1930s you could rent one of these houses for 4 or 5 shillings a week.

A scene still recognisable today even though these houses have been demolished. The stone pillar in the foreground still stands although the gas lamp has long gone. The first house in this dropped footpath (which led to Mill Street, emerging by the Ragged School), was occupied by the Hughes family.

This passageway was known locally as the Gulley or sometimes as Slaughter House Gulley. The slaughter house was behind some cottages which stood on the right of the passageway. It belonged to Bayley's butchers of Derby Street. Next to the slaughter house was Bayley & Morris, builders and joiners. The small building in the photograph with a large door and a pitched roof still stands; the inscription on this building reads "Belle Vue Dyeworks, 1928".

An aerial view of the West End with Westwood Recreation Ground (known as the Rec) clearly shown. This 5-acre Recreation Ground was laid out between Westwood Road and Spring Gardens in 1879. Note the lack of properties in Sneyd Street and Sneyd Avenue which were not built until the 1930s (top right hand corner).

Top left: This row of seven houses stood in front of the slaughter house. In the 1960s the slaughter house was a milk dairy which was eventually taken over by Mountside Dairy. The rear of Big Mill may be seen on the extreme left.

Left: A different perspective of the same houses. Above them are two buildings which were at one time part of Wardle & Davenports. Today the long building is a fireplace factory and the taller building is used by Churnetside Joinery.

Children having fun at the Westwood Rec in 1894. A timeless scene which could relate to any decade. The maypole-type apparatus was known as the Giant's Stride.

The early years of the 20th century in Westwood Road. This road was rather select and the houses mainly occupied by the middle class.

Smartly dressed children play on the swings at Westwood Rec c. 1894, watched by a bare footed boy.

Also having fun at the drinking fountain in the Rec are Bruce and Jet who belonged to Shenton's and Starlings, respectively. This photograph was taken in the 1950s.

Left: Looking towards Westwood Road from the Rec which still retained its border of iron railings. The railings were removed during World War II; you can still see the cut-off ends of the railings in the wall opposite the Westwood Road houses.

Below left: James Street laid out in 1901 by James Cornes a Leek builder. It is thought that two of the streets built by Mr Cornes were named after two of his sons namely James and Langford. The 50 workers houses erected in these streets had been built to a design of JT Brearley. Hulme's shop on the corner is now occupied by Mr Elkin, a craftsman upholsterer.

Below: Cruso Street on what looks like Club Day. Everybody is turned out in their best clothes for the event. The street on the right is the bottom of John Street. The first banner is from one of the town's Friendly Societies. What has happened to all the old banners? If they survive, they would make an interesting exhibition.

Here is The Field, better known as Field House in use as a private residence. It is now in High Street, but formerly its grounds stretched to Strangman Street and between Salisbury Street and the rear of the properties fronting St. Edward Street.

This early 19th century house was built for brothers William and Samuel Phillips who were silk manufacturers. After the brothers died, the house was occupied by Thomas and Catherine Whittles and their family. The beginning of the 20th Century saw the grounds of Field House sold for housing. In later years, this house was used as a registration centre for enlistment in World War I. It has been run as a temperance hotel and is now Leek National Reserve club.

The premises now occupied by the Leek Post & Times was formerly a workhouse and later Clowes' dyehouse. Built in 1768, in Spout Lane, it gave its name to Workhouse Street which in turn became Brook Street. The workhouse was enlarged so that by 1834, it was four-storeys high. At this time it had about 54 inmates who were fed and clothed for 3/6d each a week. The children were employed in the Leek silk mills. A new workhouse was built on Ashbourne Road in 1839 (often referred to as "251") and became the Moorlands Hospital in 1948. Prior to 1768, the workhouse was in the building used by Morton's jewellers in Derby Street, prior to its demolition in 1965 (see page 87, Volume 1).

Mrs Eaton stands in the doorway of Carding's grocery shop in Brook Street. Cornerhouse Antiques today occupies these premises and is indeed on the corner of Brook Street and Compton. In this early photograph other properties stand below Carding's shop. The building, on the extreme right is the 'Lord Raglan' public house which was demolished in order to widen the approach to Compton.

An artist's impression of the community of houses which comprised Step Row, Joliffe and Cornhill Streets. Mr George Oultram who lived at 3, Cornhill Street as a young child painted this picture which shows Step Row in the centre foreground, with Joliffe Street running up from the steps in Brook Street. Cornhill Street was round the corner from Joliffe Street and part of it still survives.

Far left: Climbing the Cornhill Steps from Brook Street

Left: Emily and Jim Carding with their Mother Catherine, in the doorway of 8, Joliffe Street. The photograph dates from 1912 and sadly Catherine Carding died while her husband James was on active service in France. These two small children were cared for by aunts, who lived in the area, until their father came home from the war.

This lovely study of Mr Webb and a cat was taken at the top of the Cornhill Steps. It portrays the properties in Joliffe Street, with part of Job White's mill at the rear.

From Joliffe Street looking over the roof tops of the town towards St Edward's Church. The houses have long since gone and we don't often see a motor bike and sidecar these days.

It's 1976 and the houses in Joliffe Street are boarded up prior to demolition. Fred Eaton and his cousin Jim Carding take a last nostaligic look at an area which held so many memories for them.

These properties in Cornhill Street were destroyed by the disasterous fire at Job White's mill in 1964 and had to be demolished.

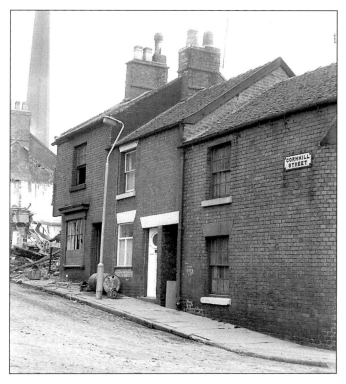

Fred Eaton and Jim Carding outside their grandfather's house in Cornhill Street. The houses to the right of the photograph still stand and are occupied today. These houses, numbered 17 to 25 Cornhill Street, were occupied in 1881 by Joseph Mould, a bricklayer, Joseph Birchenough, a silk twister, John Lalley, a labourer, Joseph Knight, an engine tenter and James Johnson, a railway signalman. John Lalley who hailed from Ireland lived at no 21 with his wife and six children and James Johnson at no 25 had 5 children. These small terraced houses held not only wives and children but also mother-in-laws and boarders!

Prospect Place and the corner of Cornhill Street prior to the fire at the adjacent mill of Job White & Co.

These houses in Compton appear to have silk twisters shades on their upper storeys. These were long rooms stretching over the attics of several houses. As early as 1817, Compton was the name given to this northern part of the Cheddleton Road. The houses were demolished in 1965. See also page 133 re the left hand side.

Compton with Job White's Mill and Prospect Place to the left. Behind the corner of Compton and Duke Street stood a court known as O' Donnells Yard or Square. It was a court off Compton approached through an entry opposite the Green Man public house. The entry can be seen on this photograph. In 1857 a report by a medical committee set up to investigate Leek's high mortality rate described O' Donnells Square as being a system of building outrageous to the sense of the 19th century. The properties were owned by White's Mill and were demolished after the mill fire in 1964. There is a report that the area between London Bank and Compton included a huge cesspit into which, presumably, O' Donnells Square and adjacent houses were drained. Apparently an elephant from a travelling circus died near here and ended its days in the cesspit.

Duke Street properties, now also demolished.

This interesting view taken from Broad Street shows the backs of the houses in Joliffe Street standing high above Compton.

Leek's Butter Cross in the Cemetery prior to its restoration to the Market Place where it rightly belonged.

Rural tranquility as sedate strollers leisurely amble along a leafy Newcastle Road. It is not like this today!

Left: Spooner's Lane became Canal Street after a branch canal from Endon to Leek was opened in 1801. The road was lowered on two separate occasions resulting in the deep cuttings seen today. Canal Street was so narrow in places that two carts had difficulty in passing; it was widened and renamed Broad Street. This interesting old house stood on the ground where Mellor's Garage was eventually built. The roof is falling in and a workman is perched on the ridge, whether to effect repairs or to dismantle the roof cannot be ascertained. A large hole to the side of the property is appropriately fenced off. The two large terraced properties above this old house have also been demolished. Thomas Grace, the well known builder and contractor, lived in one of these houses. His builders yard was also in Broad Street. Thomas Street and Grace Street were named after him.

Below left: cobbles cover the road in Broad Street. This photograph was taken on a quiet day. This street was usually busy as travellers, tradesmen and animals made their way into the town after disembarking at the Railway Station. The Sentinel Branch Office on the corner is better known, locally, as Cooper's newsagents. The tall building further up, on the same side, bears the words 'Hambleton and Sons, House Furnishers' – Samuel Hambleton and Sons were cabinet makers here, at 52, Broad Street, for many years. They had previously had premises in West Street and Stanley Street. Their furniture warehouse still stands, but is now a fish and chip shop.

Above: the former gas works situated opposite the Churnet Valley Hotel. The whole complex, including the gasometer has now disappeared, having stopped production in October, 1964.

Leek Gas Light Company began in 1826 and shortly afterwards was providing gas for just over a hundred gas lamps in Leek. Half of these lamps were lit from dusk until 2am and the other half lit from dusk until 6am. In the interest of economy none of them were lit in the three nights before a full moon or for one night after! Mr Richard Badnall at his factory in Mill Street was the first person to use gas in Leek. The fumes from the works were thought to bring relief in the cure of whooping cough and many young children were perambulated between the Railway Station and the canal to inhale the obnoxious fumes.

Two views of Wallbridge Farm which was opposite the entrance to the Wallbridge housing estate.
This farm existed by 1775 and was demolished in 1974 to make way for the Barnfields Industrial Estate.
Many people will remember the Salt family who farmed here.

Leek Wharf. The Trent and Mersey Canal Co opened a branch from the Caldon
Canal at Endon to Leek. This was in 1801 and the canal ended in the basin and wharf
in Leek pictured here near the Newcastle Road. Narrow boats carried coal into Leek
and many coal merchants operated from the Wharf. These included Charles Fogg,
Nathan Goodfellow, R. & M. A. Hall, John Potts & Co, James Goodwin, Henry
William Nixon, Henry Machin and William Scotton. Coal continued to be brought
into Leek by canal until 1834. Tar continued to be delivered here from Milton until
1939.

The canal wharf in later years after it had been filled in. The site had been purchased by Leek Urban District Council in 1957. Here it is occupied by Bowyer's scrapyard.

The Leek arm of the Caldon canal which ended in the basin and wharf off the Newcastle Road.

In 1849 the North Staffordshire Railway Company opened a station at Leek on the Newcastle Road. Leek Station was designed by William Sugden, a Yorkshireman, who had come to Leek as a surveyor and architect of the Churnet Valley Railway Line.

In the earlier view (above) carriages line up outside the station in the snow ready to transport weary passengers into Leek; perhaps to one of the four commercial hotels: The Red Lion, Swan, George & Roebuck.

A busy scene outside the station

Porters and passengers jostle together as they wait for the shuddering, reverberating, hissing steam train to rush into the station. The platform is crowded; probably it's Market day!

To the right of the photograph is the narrow up-platform. By todays standards it appears rather dangerous, especially on busy days.

A five-coach passenger train leaves Leek, heading south. This portrays the old station very well in halçon days of the mid-20th Century.

UTTOXETER, CHURNET LINE, MACCLESFIELD AND MANCHESTER

Weekdays only

		a.m	a.m	a.m	SO a.m	SO p.m	WO p.m	SO p.m	p.m	p.m	SX p.m	SO p.m
Uttoxeter	dep.	620	655	819	1145	...	250	3 0	440	...	6 0	610
Rocester		627	7 3	827	1152	...	257	3 7	448	...	6 7	617
Denstone		630	7 6	829	1155	...	3 0	310	451	...	610	620
Alton Towers		636	712	835	12 1	...	3 6	316	457	...	616	626
Oakamoor		642	717	839	12 5	...	310	320	5 4	...	621	631
Kingsley & Froghall		648	723	844	1211	...	316	326	511	...	627	637
Consall		653	728	849	1216	...	321	331	516	...	632	642
Cheddleton		658	733	854	1221	...	326	336	520	...	636	646
Leek	arr.	7 5	740	9 1	1228	...	333	343	527	...	643	653
Leek	dep.	7 8	751	910	1232	136	336	346	...	6 0	648	658
Rudyard Lake		711	754	913	1235	139	339	349	...	6 3	651	7 1
Cliffe Park Halt		...	8 0	...	1241	145	345	355	...	6 9	...	...
Rushton		719	8 5	920	1245	149	348	358	...	612	7 0	710
Bosley		724	810	926	1250	154	354	4 3	...	617	...	...
North Rode		728	814	932	1257	159	358	4 7	...	621	7 8	718
Macclesfield (Central)	arr.	737	823	...	1 6	2 8	4 7	416	...	630	717	727
Macclesfield (Hibel Road)	arr.	7A50	825	941	1 8	210	4 9	418	...	632	719	729
Stockport (Edgeley)	arr.	8F26	9 5	1025	147	325	514	514	...	725	752	825
Manchester (London Road)	arr.	8F38	914	1034	156	342	5B30	530	...	740	8 6	840

A—Change at Macclesfield (Central). F—On Sats. arr. Stockport 8-15 a.m., Manchester (Mayfield) 8-24 a.m.
SO—Saturdays only. WO—Wednesdays only. B—Manchester (Mayfield).

The Churnet Valley railway timetable from the early 1960s PMT bus timetable. What a pity this timetable from Leek Station is not operable today. You could travel quite easily to Alton Towers in just over half an hour

Above: between the station and Two Arches Bridge stood the signal box. Peeping out behind the box is one of the council houses on Junction Road.

Below: weeds flourish on the platform, debris lies on the lines, buildings are neglected and abandoned. The station was left high and dry after being axed in the first week of 1964. What a difference it would have made to our congested journeys to work if we could have let the train take the strain. These photographs were taken shortly before demolition.

More views of the deserted, derelict station.

Above: the down platform

Below: the water tower; with the waterpipe for replenishing the locos and the view towards the signalbox & Two Arches Bridge

Middle: the former turning circle – it clearly had not been used for years.

A standard class 4 No 75030 leaves Leek Yard on 9th September 1966.

The same train passing the Cattle Market on its way towards Leekbrook Junction. Both of these views were taken from Two Arches Bridge.

2-6-0, No 42828 leaves Leek for Macclesfield and was photographed passing the gas works.

Taken on Maundy Thursday, 1928, this ex-NSR 2-4-2 tank is shown here as LMS No 1457. It was a passenger train and was bound for Stoke-on-Trent.

Another photograph from 1928; on 11th July, Gordon Walwyn took this photograph of 0-6-0 No 8511.

This excursion train (bound for Blackpool via Stoke on Trent) leaves Leek headed by a Stanier Black Five, No 45084, its safety valves beginning to lift from a full head of steam.

A Stanier Class 5, 4-6-0, No 45096 with a mixed load of passengers and freight rolling stock leaving Leek.

In BR days, a three coach set pulled by another Stanier loco on a lovely summers day.

Leek's last blacksmith. Many people will remember the days when this busy smithy in Ashbourne Road would have two horses being shod inside while two or three more awaited their turn in the yard. John Meakin and his brother Fred who worked here shoed farm horses and painted farm carts. The gaily painted carts were famous all over the Staffordshire Moorlands.

Arthur Goldstraw, a telegraph boy. Prior to the telephone system, urgent messages were sent by telegraph and were relayed to the recipient by bike. What a change from the mass communications of today which we take for granted. Arthur was born in 1905.

A familiar sight not too many years ago as a chimney sweep cycles along Junction Road. The sweep pictured here is Mr William Turner who was a Leek builder, the chimney sweeping was merely a sideline!

Painters working for the Council pause in their labours, momentarily, for a photograph!

Arthur Goldstraw features here too. He is on the far right and took the photograph, his duties as a telegraph boy just a memory! (See page 95).

Another group of painters including Syd Goldstraw (see page 96), so this may be Phillips's workforce (? at Westwood Hall).

These painters, posed more formally, were working
for Edwin Phillips, master painter and decorator.
Back row: E Brown, Fred D Brassington, Sydney
Goldstraw (Arthur's brother) and G Copping;
Middle row: H Ball, N Trafford; Front row: Joe
Challinor, T Provost and B Meredith.

A group of workmen erecting York Mill in Well Street in 1898. Note the wooden scaffolding and lack of protective headgear. Two of the men standing on the scaffolding are Jack Johnson and Abraham Pickford. Abraham died just one year later in 1899 aged just 26. He was the father of Lorenzo Pickford who served with the Leek Battery. The small boy on the extreme left is Bert Ralphs, then aged 7, he lived in Wood Street. Among the other workmen are Tom Buxton, Harry Biddulph, a stonemason of Nelson Street, Joseph Heywood, a bricklayer and brothers Jack and Philip Hamilton also bricklayers.

An unknown group of Leek workmen. It is not known whether they are erecting or dismantling the building or where the photograph was taken. Any information would be appreciated by the authors.

A fine fowl for a lady's delectation. Baskets abound underneath this cart in Derby Street. The shops across the street are built onto the front of 13, Derby Street. This site is now occupied by Boots the Chemists. Perhaps this photograph more than most in this book captures the Spirit of Leek in the early years of the 20th century, along with the photograph below.

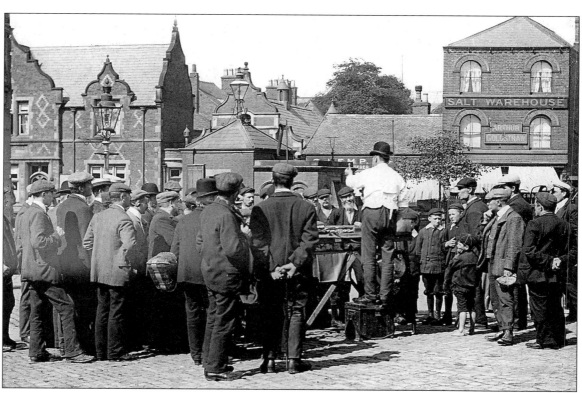

Will they buy or are they just enjoying the patter? This group of men are gathered at the bottom of Derby Street where a cheap-jack is touting his wares. Whatever he is selling is obviously of no interest to a lady! Notice the boy with no shoes.

A weary horse and an equally tired coal man take a well earned breather while delivering coal in Station Street.

Not the most salubrious of jobs but it achieved fame on BBC's 'What's My Line?' This fine fellow is washing the tails of cows at Leek's cattle market!

From 1870, Leek's fire engine was housed in the premises pictured here in Stockwell Street. The buildings were part of the Cock Inn, whose stables stretched from the corner of the Market Place down Stockwell Street. Here the firemen are smartly turned out in their best uniform and boots and wearing their heavy brass helmets. On the ladder are H Alcock and W Davenport. Standing on the engine are two members of the Carding family, W Wilshaw and 2nd Eng Jones. Front row l-r: H Buxton, V Carding, W Wood, A Carding, AV Holton, Lt Clowes, Cpt Wardle, Cpt Carding, Dr Hammersley, WB Nadin, T Alcock and H Billing. This photograph was taken in the closing days of the old fire station.

Although this photograph is slightly out of focus it has been included because of its interest. As bandsmen, dance troupes and people in fancy dress can be seen, it is presumed that this may be a carnival occasion. Taken around 1928, the girls in their flapper-style dresses and headgear seem to be carrying American style pom poms. As the girls are not dancing and  the band isn't playing, the cameraman seems to have caught a lull in the proceedings. The fire engine with its number plate E9883 may be the motor engine bought in 1924 and nicknamed 'Wilson' after the chairman of the fire brigade committee. The driver of the vehicle is F Wright and seated beside him is Horace Pickford. Standing on the running board is Captain Carding and firemen travelling on the engine include Malkin, B Lockett, C Parker and R Wheeldon. The view is near the junction of Garden Street with Belle Vue.

Carnival Day again, this time in 1930, and Leek firemen are once more part of the procession as it travels down Buxton Road. The driver is still F Wright, beside him is Vic Carding and standing to his right is Arthur Foster. The firemen on the vehicle are Messrs Malkin, Pickford, Heywood and Plant.

Posing in the Market Place in the mid 30s are F Wright, A Foster, Malkin, C Parker, J Banks, R Weildon, H Pickford, H Hulstone, B Lockett and H Noble.

Leek firemen stand smartly to attention as they are inspected during the years of World War II. This inspection took place at the rear of the Fire Station in the Red Lion Yard.

A dramatic view of firemen fighting the fire at Mayers' Euston Mill in Wellington Street. The white building on the right is the Wellington Inn. Strangman Street is chaotically choked with fire fighters' vehicles as the men struggled to contain the blaze. The mill chimney is lit up by the fire which destroyed the mill.

The previous photographs of Leek firemen show them on parade or taking part in joyous festivities, but of course, they had a dangerous and difficult job. Apart from being called out to domestic properties they were involved in fighting the massive infernoes which raged through many of Leek's textile mills (see opposite).

Here firemen are pictured tackling a blaze in Plant's furniture store in St Edward Street. They are fighting the fire from the yard behind the Wilkes' Head in the area which is now the car park off High Street. Firemen are on the ground and on the roof while two others train water on the blaze from the Simon Snorkel high above the ground. They are almost enveloped in the cloud of steam emanating from the mix of fire and water.

Leek Ambulance Brigade was formed in August 1915, meeting in the Carr Gymnasium on Stockwell Street. At first the brigade was comprised of men who worked at railway stations in Leek and the surrounding district. The railway companies at that time being keen to encourage their workforce to take up first aid work. After appealing in the local press, others joined and the Leek St John's Ambulance Brigade was formed.

This, taken in 1916 shortly after the brigade was formed, includes John Wood, Leek Stationmaster, Mr Shufflebotham, Joseph Lovatt, William Hassall, Doctor Burnett, Police Sergeant Morton and Samuel Godwin.

The St Johns Ambulance Brigade in December 1940.

E9817 was on the number plate of Leek's new ambulance which was presented to the town by the hospital convalescent committee. Prior to this Leek had a motor ambulance for non-infectious and accident cases and a horse drawn vehicle for infectious cases. Kathleen Pickford remembers when, as a child with diptheria, she was transported to the isolation hospital in Ashbourne Road in this fearsome vehicle with the blinds drawn firmly down! After the purchase of the new ambulance in 1924, the old horse drawn vehicle was no longer used; the infectious cases now using the older motor ambulance. In these early years it was part of the Leek firemens job to drive the ambulance.

Sister Margaret Hall, district midwife, out on her rounds in the late 1950s. Margaret had earlier nursed at Leek Moorlands Hospital and in later years became a school nurse.

John Bagnall was the proprietor of the Queen Laundry in 1904. The laundry was in Cruso Street and was still operating there in 1912, although its name had changed to Imperial & Queen Laundries Ltd.

Pictured here is Adams Butter's first mobile show trailer. Standing by the trailer, which is in front of Ball Haye Hall, are Lynton Goldstraw, Basil Blore and Jack Chester.

Two views of the Midland Bank in days gone by, plus a bewhiskered fireman waiting for the next callout.

A study full of character: a nightwatchman, snug in his shelter, patiently endures the long night hours warmed by his brazier.

Left: two workmen take time out with their dog for company.

Below: four fine fellows taking a break from work at Tatton's despatch bay at their Buxton Road works. Second from left is Len Sheldon, followed by Harry Mace and Horace Moreton.

The schools of the town are a rich source of photographs for a book such as this.
We have tried to show a selection across the last one hundred years or so. This is not only to
try and be representative of each generation but also to show changes in fashions and styles
of clothing. In some of the earlier photographs, it is possible that many of the children
portrayed have passed on, but we hope that the images of innocent faces bring back
memories to some and recognition of parents and grandparents to others.

St Edwards Hall, c. 1986. From left to right are:
Front Row: Steph Taylor, Rachel Binns, Mathew Knowles, ... Sheila Farley, Sammy Smith;
2nd Row: Joanne Kirkham, ?, Louise Jones, Helen Rowley, Joanne Burndred, Venessa
Beech, ?, Maureen Salt, ?, Rebecca Lisle, Louise Beeby, Rachel Chadwick;
3rd Row: 6th from left – Nick Whittingham, Jeremy Worth, Lucy Hutchinson, ?, Karen
Bevington;
4th Row: ?, Kim Tatton, Ruth Goodwin, Helen Rigby, ?, ?, Joanne Nadin, Mary Price,
Denise ?, Vicky Ward, Nicola Ellis, Mike Gledhill;
Back Row: ?, Paul Lovatt, ?, Graham Knight & Sarah Tatton (now married to one another),
Sarah West, Anthony Knight, Peter Whittaker, ?, ?, ?.

Pupils at All Saints School pictured about 1905. The boy in the centre of the middle row is Sidney Simpson, his brother Percy is seated on the front row, fourth from the left. Also present are teachers Miss Elsie Bradley and Miss Gibson together with the headmaster of the school Mr W A Furmston. At this time there were over 400 children attending at this school.

All Saints C.E. (Aided) First school affectionately known as Compton School. After opening as a church-cum-school in 1863, services continued to be held here until All Saints Church was built in 1887. The building was extended over several decades from 1872 to 1891. A plaque read "Christ Church School, AD 1872". After years of overcrowding and maintenance difficulties the number of pupils fell to less than 150 by the early 1960s. A new school was erected further down the road in 1964/65 at a cost of £57,000. The old school has recently been demolished and housing erected on the site by Colin Amos, a local builder.

Over seventy years separate these photographs of pupils who attended St Luke's School. The earlier photograph taken about 1908 depicts rather glum faced children, standing smartly to attention. The pupils who attended the school in 1980 are much more cheerful and relaxed. Is this a sign of less strict discipline or simply advances in photography?

St Luke's National Schools opened in 1847 in Fountain Street. A new school designed by William Sugden opened in 1872; this school had entrances from Queen Street and Earl Street. The new school was exclusively for boys when first opened but mixed classes were held there after 1893. Some 256 pupils were on the register at St Luke's in 1931 but the numbers dwindled in the following years. The school closed in 1981 just after this photograph was taken.

Mr Parker was the headmaster at West Street School when these two photographs were taken. Details regarding this school can be found in the section on 'The West End' in this volume.

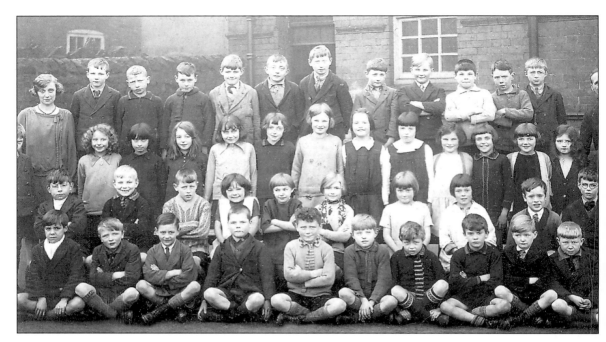

Pupils at West Street School in 1930, the children are about 9 years of age. In this class photograph are Miss Meakin (teacher), Denis Knowles, Eric Hill, Georgie Graham, Eric Butterworth, Basil Turner, Ron Wilshaw, Len Tunnicliffe, Raymond Morris, Doreen Keates, Stella Perkin, Eileen Houlihan, Joyce Brentnall, Enid Pickering and Roy Hulme.

Only a few of the pupils at West Street School have been named in this photograph also taken about 1930. They are Ken Turner, Bert Smith, Les Oliver and Jackie Belfield. Miss Ball was the lady teacher and George Henry Mason the headmaster. Both these photographs were taken in the girl's playground and the upper one shows the houses in West Street Square in the left background.

Pupils at Miss Marsland's School in Union Street. These youngsters who are nicely dressed and appear to come from more affluent families are pictured in a garden. Was Miss Marsland's a private school? Perhaps so, but a certain young lady in Edwardian times was told by her mother that she could not go to Miss Marsland's school because she only taught an ordinary education, dancing and manners! In 1904, Miss Marsland was living at 27, Queen Street and listed as a private resident in Kelly's directory of that year. The working classes were never listed in this section. Not many years after this photograph was taken the school closed and a box making business was set up in the vacated schoolroom in Union Street.

Miss Raynor's School at 18, Moorfields was a private school. The children whom she taught were the sons and daughters of professional people. The names of Leek mill owners and businessmen are easily recognized in the names of these young pupils. *Back Row:* John Richard Hough, Tony Davenport, Charles Bradshaw, ? Argles. *Middle Row:* Gerald Mee, Valentine Worthington, ? , Elwyn Blades, John Cowlishaw. *Front Row:* David Watson, John Arundel, Philip Worthington, John Haigh, Yvonne Birch, ?.

Britannia Street School about 1918. This school evolved from St Edward's National School on Clerk Bank. The boys moved to the new school in Britannia Street in 1886. The girls and infants who had been left in the Clerk Bank building also moved to Britannia Street when the school on Clerk Bank finally closed in 1894. The Clerk Bank school then became the Maude Institute. Both the Maude Institute and the Britannia Street School building still stand, the former is used for meetings and events of all kinds and the latter is now a fitness centre and beauticians. Pupils pictured here in 1918 include Gladys Lee and Tom Knight. Standing on the right is John Alsop who taught Maths at the school.

Children on this Britannia Street class photograph include Jack Reeves, Hilda Cantrell, Elsie Lee, Len Hollinshead, Bill Fowler, Ernie Tunnicliffe, Arthur Torkington and Ken Hopkinson. Girls and boys had different playgrounds at this time and the sexes were separated in other ways. In Hargreaves School at the bottom of Alsop Street, the girls were taught cookery and household chores in a room upstairs while the boys had woodwork lessons on the ground floor!

Boys at Britannia Street were also taught gardening skills in the school garden which was off Beggars Lane and adjacent to Pegg's Nursery garden. Digging and delving here in 1927 are:- *Back Row:* Hill, G Hill, R Birch, Sam Scholes (headmaster), J Alsop (assistant head master). *Middle Row:* W Bennion, R Renshaw, Sigley, H Plant, Belfield. *Front Row:* E Tunnicliffe, W Brough, J Fowler, Ken Bowyer, L Hollinshead.

Britannia Street School in the 1920s. Pupils include Billie Bennion, Harold Plant, Ron Birch, Ernie Tunnicliffe, Ken Bowyer, Mabel Pickford, Len Hollinshead, George Hill, Flossie Birch, Ron Renshaw and Jack Fowler. The young woman is the teacher, a Miss Yarwood.

A group of children at Britannia Street in 1928. *Back row includes:* Kenneth James, Phyllis Green, Kathleen Sheldon, Stuart Macmillan. *4th row includes:* Victor Abbott, Adella Miller, Philip Swindlehurst. *3rd row includes:* Barbara Jackson, Norman Wright, Doreen Guilliard. *2nd row includes:* Arnold Beardmore and Douglas Birks *Front row includes:* Stanley Walters and Roy Campion. Norman Wright was four years old when this photograph was taken. When he was seven he had to go to West Street as Britannia Street became a secondary school. Norman returned to Britannia Street when he reached eleven years of age.

Pupils pose in the Salisbury Street playground in 1936. The Palace Picture House was beyond the wall on the corner of High Street. This former bowling alley and cinema is now a Salvation Army Citadel.

Another view of Britannia Street School. This photograph was taken c.1930. Lindsey Porter's father, Stanley, born in 1918, is first on the left, 2nd row from front.

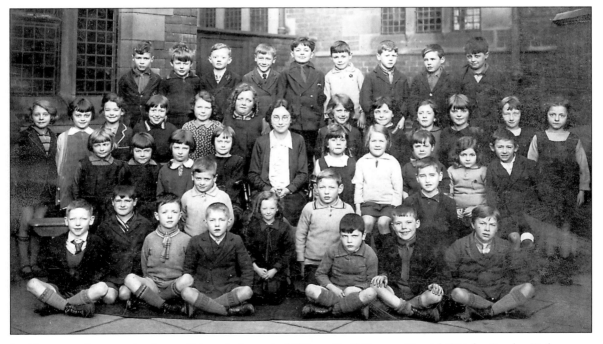

In this group photograph taken at Britannia Street in 1935 are Basil Cooper, Derrick Wright, Stanley Hulme, Kathleen Pickford, Miss Walker, Dennis Hambleton, Anson Moss, Eric Tyler, Joan Matthews, Doris Alcock, Mary Smith and Fred Torkington.

As part of the coronation celebrations in 1937, local schools staged a series of historical tableaux. The Romans and Queen Boudicea was the tableau presented by pupils of the Parish Church Senior School. East Street School (below) began life as Leek Council Schools. It opened in 1914 and was extended in 1927. The senior school

moved to Springfield Road in 1937 leaving 150 children at East Street in the infants department. By 1940 East Street was the towns largest primary school with over 400 pupils on the register. New extensions which were added in 1966/7 and the opening of other schools in Leek eased the overcrowding situation in the school. After accommodating over 500 children in the 1950s the numbers dropped to around 200 by the late 80s. East Street is now a first school where pupils attend between the ages of five and nine.

East Street 1932. *Back Row:* Vic Bailey, Roy Clowes, Brian Nicholas, Fred Brassington, Stanley Knott, Derrick Edge, Stanley Reid, Harold Goldstraw, Colin Spencer, Alfred Heath
3rd Row: Irene Greenwood, Joan Gittins, Joan Fogg, Joan Trafford, Florence Yeomans, Margaret Cooper, Doris Wain, Brenda Dix, Cecily Keates, Joyce Goodfellow, Elsie Quick, Dorothy Gee
2nd Row: Bernard Corden, Lily Price, Joan Clowes, Katherine Stubbs, Annie Edwards, Joan Birch, Francis Meakin, Betty Prince, Barbara Walker, Leonard Clowes
Front row: Clifford Lovenbury, Arthur Fisher, Arthur Schofield, Robert Poyser.

East Street 1936. *Back row:* Jack Harrison, Fred Brassington, Jack Berrisford, Eddie Loton, Derek Hill, Jess Knott, Doris Wain, Francis Harrison. *Middle Row:* Joyce Rider, May Worthington, Joan Birch, May Rowlinson, Irene Greenwood, Muriel Hilton, Ivy Hall, Dorothy Graham, Kathleen Healy, Dorothy Berresford, Gladys Hodgkinson, Joyce Lomas, Mary Lowe. *Front Row:* Tom Jenkins, Eric Duffin, Bertram Sheldon, Desmond Bishop, Norman Beardmore, Leonard Oliver.

East Street, 1958. *Front Row:* ? Elizabeth Allen, Yvonne Porter, Pat Rowlinson, Dorothy Allen, Elizabeth Shenton, Maureen Barnet, Helen Hurd, Pam Richardson, Christine Lovatt, Julie Wardle, Christine Smith. *Middle Row:* Robin Richmond, Roy Williams, Pamela Knott, Mavis Birch, Gillian Wilson, Pat Campion, Sylvia Fowler, Gillian Poyser, Susan Turner, Pat Bradbury, Jill Hulme, Judith Braddock, Christine Shenton, Maureen Dale, Lindsey Porter. *Back Row:* John Tatton, Andrew McFadden, John Alcock, David Kelsall, Stuart Scragg, Roger Westerman, David Smith, Christopher Rane, Jeffrey Perkin, Miss Bullock, Mrs Bentley, Michael Healey, John Swarbrook, Alec Turley, Geoffrey Plant, Richard Heath, Norman Wickstead.

Youngsters at East Street First School entertaining fellow pupils and parents in the mid 1980s.

"Children Through the Ages" a theme presented by pupils of Westwood Road County Primary School in the 1950s. The tall boy in the centre is Ralph Sharratt.

Serious expressions on the faces of these young people as they earnestly look at the camera in 1948. They were pupils of Beresford Memorial School better known as St Paul's. The school was surrounded by open countryside at this time and Cathryn Walton (nee Beech) can remember being badly frightened by the sight of a cow giving birth in a field next to the playground!

Back Row: Pamela Milward, Russell Hurst, Francis Clarke, Sandra Smith, Valerie Keates, Robert Bradley, ? , Norman Oultram, Joy Owen, Pamela Buxton;

Middle Row: Malcolm Cooper, Eileen Anslow, Norman Ainsworth, Stuart Parr, Arthur Clowes, Tommy Gallimore, ? , Kay Pickford, ? , Howard Hilton, Cockersole, Frank Rogers, peter Smith, Patrick Miles;

Front Row: Christine Corden, Adrienne Heath, Christine Bode, Pauline Kirby, Barbara Broda, Gillian Foden, Fay Milward, Cathryn Beech, Jean Tatton, Jacqueline Owen.

Pupils at Milner Girls School in Springfield Road in 1962.

Built by Thomas Joliffe, a wool merchant in 1627, this building was the Hall House. The exact date when it became the Red Lion is not known, although Joliffe sold his Staffordshire estate in 1765. In the early 19th century as many as 1,000 people would attend the Court leet held in the Red Lion Inn by the Earl of Macclesfield's steward. No doubt the event was good for socialising too. When balls were held in the Assembly Room the Market Place would be crowded with people anxious to glimpse the finery and feathers of ladies alighting from their carriages.

Young ladies would be equally keen to catch the eye of officers, in their colourful uniforms, who used the Red Lion as a 'mess' when troops passed through the town. On a more sombre note, a tragedy occurred here in 1836 when a traveller from Brazil shot himself shortly after leaving the 'Defiance' stagecoach.

When Mr Swift was the landlord in the early 1900s the family couch in the coffee room was upholstered with the hair of their pet pony whose tail hung from the centre of the seat at the end! In more recent years dinners and dances have been held here, travellers have been accommodated and townsfolk have quenched their thirst at the bar. After a period of neglect, the Red Lion has emerged from its dilapidated hibernation and is once again a popular social centre for the people of Leek.

The rear of the Red Lion with a cart and carriage standing on the cobbled Red Lion yard.

Inside the Red Lion between the wars as ladies attend an American Tea. The ladies would meet for refreshments and bring along items for sale. Mrs Annie Mee inaugurated these occasions; she had taken over the Red Lion after the death of her husband in 1918. She was assisted by her son Charles Mee and his wife Mary.

Distinguished gentleman at a dinner in the Red Lion about 1918. Among those present were Stuart McKenzie, Colonel A.F. Nicholson, Philip Hammersley, Charles Henry Lee, Norman Thompson and Dennis Fallon. On the back wall hangs a portrait of Charles Gerald Mee, husband of Annie, and grandfather of Gerald Mee. The gas light fitting on the ceiling was replaced by electric light in 1925, just in time for Gerald's christening.

The Bird in Hand stands at the corner of Market Place and Sheepmarket. This Elizabethan style building was erected in 1889 replacing the original Bird in Hand. This former pub had been a 'a low black and white-washed house' which had very low rooms and was considered to be very unhealthy. The landlord of the newly built Bird in Hand was Thomas Bolstridge.

The Duke of York Inn at 51, Derby Street. This public house occupied this site from as early as 1793. The building is set back from the line of Derby Street as can be seen from the cobbled forecourt. Later photographs show that the cobbles were replaced by paving stones. Market stalls were erected on this forecourt. It no doubt brought in extra customers to the pub. The coach to Buxton set off from here (see p. 91 of Volume 1). In 1881 James and Maria Walwyn ran the Duke of York with the help of their son

Fred. Today a branch of Leek United Building Society stands in this same site and is still set back from the line of other buildings in Derby Street. However the Fine Fare supermarket was the first occupier of the new building.

A coach laden with baskets stands outside the Cock Inn at 19, Derby Street. The inn has been established here by the early 19th century. In the early years of the 20th century, John Munro operated a wine and spirit business from these premises while his son Murdo Munro was the landlord. John Munro came from Tairn in the Scottish Highlands. He settled in Rudyard, building Fairview there in 1879/80. Later Munro's wine business moved to Stanley Street and was eventually taken over by John Joules brewery of Stone. When Bass bought that brewery, Munros was closed down. See page 130.

The Roebuck was one of Leek's main coaching inns. 'Telegraph' coaches called here on their journeys between London and Manchester. Together with other coaching inns in Leek the Roebuck provided accommodation for travellers and stabling for horses. According to the Victoria County History, before 1848 Russell Street was called Roebuck Lane. However, local tradition in the town differs: Roebuck Lane being the lane to Brook Street which runs down the side of the inn. The Lowndes family sold it for £4,120 in 1876. Messrs Bell and Co of Burton took over the Roebuck in 1882.

Although dated 1626, no records of an inn called the Roebuck exist until the 18th century. Recent research suggests that the inn was originally a private house.

An old advert for Munros. See also page 128 for further details of this firm.

G. & J. MUNRO & Co., Ltd.,

WHOLESALE & RETAIL

WINE, SPIRIT,

Ale & Porter Merchants,

DERBY STREET, LEEK, and

MARKET STREET, HANLEY.

SOLE AGENTS FOR

OLD GAUL,

"X X X,"
" RESERVE,"
" LIQUEUR,"

GREER'S O. V. H. WHISKY.

GOODS DELIVERED FREE TO ALL PARTS.

The Dog and Partridge seen here on the left at 11, Derby Street. To the right of the pub are the iron railings around the garden of William Sugden's house at 13, Derby Street, (now Boots Chemists). The landlord of the Dog and Partridge in 1884 was George Spilsbury; he had previously kept the Nag's Head in Mill Street. The building which housed the Dog and Partridge still survives and is now used by Timpsons Shoes and Castle Cards.

The Wilkes Head in St Edward Street, named after John Wilkes, the 18th century champion of freedom of the press. In 1841 Joseph Pickford, a victualler, lived here with his wife Elizabeth and their children Clara, Caroline, Harriet and Henry. He had previously kept public houses in Derby Street and Custard Street (now Stanley Street) and was formerly licensee of The Wheatsheaf. Members of the Mill Sawyers and Woodcutting Machinists Trade Union met at the Wilkes Head in the early 1900s.

The Cheshire Cheese once stood on the corner of Spout Street and Sheepmarket; before that it was known as the Coach and Horses. Some time before 1818 the Coach and Horses was kept by a William Critchley. An advertisement is a directory of 1904 reads:-

"Ye Olde Cheshire Cheese.
Every Accommodation and convenience for cyclists and travellers.
LARGE AND SPACIOUS SMOKE AND COMMERCIAL ROOMS.
Wines and Spirits of superior quality"

In the days of the stage coach, the coaches often overturned at the Cheshire Cheese corner resulting in serious injury and broken bones. Note the ornate railings behind the boys.

This imposing property is still situated on the corner of St Edward Street and Stanley Street. Formerly Spout Street and Custard Street. Den Engel (The Angel) serves Belgian beers and refreshments here today, but years ago this was the Wheatsheaf. Not only had it changed it's name but it also somewhat less grand being now two storeys high and not three. Years ago it boasted the longest bar in Leek. Which pub claims this now?

This photograph shows the location of the Black Lion in St Edward Street. In 1901 it was a licensed beer house, as opposed to a public house which is allowed to sell spirits. The property to the left is William Allen's house at 50, St Edwards Street; he was a well known Leek lawyer. Neither Mr Allen's house or the Black Lion survive. The headquarters of the Leek United Building stands on the site of Allen's house. The Black Lion was demolished to make the entrance to Strangman Street.

This unique photograph shows the Quiet Woman and the Unicorn before 1897. In that year the Unicorn was set back and rebuilt and the workmen can be seen preparing to start some sort of renovation. For many years John Benson was the landlord of the Unicorn at the same time being landlord of the Talbot and the Sea Lion.
In 1793 the Quiet Woman was called the Good Woman, but before that date it was the White Hart. The Quiet and Good elements of the name refer to the fact that the lady in question had no head and so could not talk! An example of early sexism! An old rhyme reads:-

"Here you may find a good woman
Faithfully portrayed from ye life
Nothing is wanting but her head
Because that turns with every wind
If the head had been left her
She would never have been good in
all her life"

The old inn sign portrayed a headless woman, with a necklet of blue beads, a white muslin dress, stockings and saucy sandals.

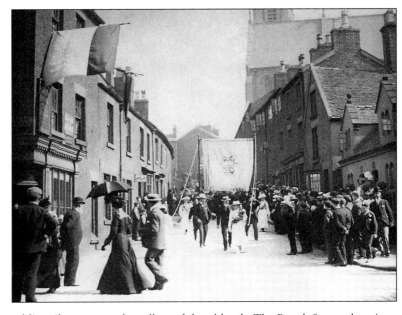

Right: the beer house on the corner of Brook Street and Compton was called the Lord Raglan Inn. Around the turn of the century Dan Chadwick was the proprietor. He had moved onto the Bull's Head in St Edward Street by 1912, presumably after the demolition of the pub and the adjacent houses. The public toilets occupy the cellars of the old pub. The Brook Street elevation of this building may be seen on the right hand side of the photograph on page 70.

The Golden Lion at 2, Church Street; another of Leek's lost inns. It existed as early as 1756 when the property was sold to William Allen, the tenant. In the years before 1780, a playhouse or clubroom was situated over a stable in the courtyard, presumably used by visiting theatre companies. William Haywood who made mineral water in Naylor yard was also the landlord of the Golden Lion in 1896. Many Leek people will nostalgically remember the days of the "Blue Room" in the late 50s and early 60s. Young people flocked to this upstairs room, overlooking the street , where they could both imbibe alcoholic beverages and listen to "pop" music. Was this Leek's first disco? This ancient hostelry was demolished in 1972, when Church Street was widened.

Through the shadowy cobbles in the archway of the Golden Lion, a timeless scene is captured on film. Carts rest on their haunches, sacks and baskets lie in abandon on the stones, people leisurely examine the wares on offer. The yard once held stables and warehouses which were used by various tradesmen over the years. The Cantrill family had a blacksmiths shop in the Golden Lion yard in the late 1800s.

The building on the extreme left is no longer with us. Situated on Clerk or School Bank, it was once kept by Uriah Davenport in the early 1800s. It was the Beehive pub.

The George was originally a coaching inn built in the 1760s on the corner of Spout Street. Coaches travelling between London and Manchester would call at the George every day.

Many travellers regarded this establishment as the most comfortable coaching house between Leek and Manchester. By 1887, the George was one of four commercial hotels in Leek, the others being the Red Lion, Roebuck and the Swan. Times changed and by 1906 the George was advertised as a family and commercial hotel and boasted that a bus met all trains. Mrs Platt was the proprietor at the time. A few years later Japeth Abbott was a brewer operating from the George. As the years passed the George became less of a hotel and more of a social venue. Leek people used it not only for the consumption of alchohol but also as a meeting place and for discos and dances.

The Swan, Leeks oldest pub, dispensing ale for some 400 years. It was previously the Green Dragon and then the Swan With Two Necks, which originated from the two nicks on the beak of some of the birds.

The Wellington standing at the corner of Wellington street and Strangman Street. Its address at 104, Strangman Street indicates that the entrance to the pub was in Strangman Street and not Wellington Street. In fact the Wellington Street part of the property was added when houses were acquired in that street. In 1898 it was kept by William Henry Peach who was president of "Leek and District Licensed Victuallers and Wine and Beersellers Friendly and Protection Society". Mr Peach plied his trade at various pubs having previously kept a beerhouse in Mill Street and the Duke of York in Derby Street. For many years in the 20th century the Wellington was kept by Richard Millard.

Audrey and Malcolm Woodings – mine hosts at the Wellington for 22 years. They took over the inn in 1976.

The Britannia Inn in West Street. In Victorian times it was kept for a while by a Mr Wardle who became a partner in Wardle and Davenport's mill.

The Black Swan in Sheepmarket gave an alternative venue to The Cheshire Cheese (see page 131) and the Bird in Hand (see page 127). It has a cruck frame, pointing to great antiquity.

A snowy scene in Stanley Street, once known as Custard Street. The hanging sign denotes the situation of the Queens Head now renamed " The Valiant". In 1837, George Walker was the landlord here as wall as acting as agent for Cheddleton Brewery. Nearly one hundred years later Thomas Pickford was a barman here. Queens Square, behind the Queens Head contained a house; a warehouse and workshops. These were advertised for sale in 1828.

The Sea Lion was eatablished between the years 1838 and 1888. In the late 19th and early 20th centurys, this public house was one of three licensed to John Benson. Herbert Moreton and Daniel Higson were two of the landlords of the Sea Lion in the first half of the 20th century. People pause to peruse the antics of a "bear", which seems to have human feet! Little has changed in this photograph today, the mill is still there as is the building on the left. However, keen observers will note that the Sea Lion has grown! There are now two sets of windows below the door as an extension has been added.

This early 19th century inn at what was London Road has many interesting and unusual architectural features. There is much to admire in the detail and design of the building. Early landlords of the Talbot were Richard Ratcliffe, T.S. Fernihough and John Weston. Meetings of the Oddfellows, Grand Union, Moorlands Lodge were held here for many years. Notice the car ignoring the roundabout!

Leek Volunteer Bandsmen march past the Talbot down down the cobbles of the London Road. The Coffee Tavern can be seen on the right.

The Talbot photographed the day after a fire in the 1990s destroyed the roof. This popular public house has since been restored to its former glory.

Court No 7, London Road (now Ashbourne Road) was a narrow passage, below Brough's mill, leading into Cross Street. This photograph reveals the hanging sign of the Dun Cow public house. Many years ago the pub was situated on Leek Moor. By the late 19th century, this old public house had become a common lodging house, although the stables were still used for Mr Hall's riding horses. On the 1881 census, 12 lodgers are recorded as staying in this property. The Dun Cow was demolished in the 1950s when it was owned by Brough, Nicholson and Hall, who afterwards used the site as a car park.

The Flying Horse taken early in the 20th Century from what was then the grounds of the Workhouse and is now the Moorlands Hospital.

The Pig and Whistle, an old beerhouse on the corner of Osbourne Street and Buxton Road, seen here converted into two cottages. The gate opened onto three steps which led to the front yard complete with water pumps. Previously known as the Hanging Gate and kept by William Hidderley, the hanging sign carried these words:-

"This gate hangs well and hinders none,
Refresh and pay, and travel on."

Two views of the Moss Rose Inn. In 1921, W Lumsden was the landlord and later it was kept by Harold Hall, who owned the Moorland Queen charabanc. It is not known when the building became the Moss Rose.

The Kings Arms at 81, Mill Street pictured here before it was extended and changed its name to the Jester. Nowadays the Jester incorporates the cottage in the right of the photograph at 83, Mill Street. The court between nos 81 and 83 no longer exists and the two separate building shown here are now one. Cathryn Waltons' great-grandfather lived in one of the tiny houses in this court at the side of the King's Arms. The court was nicknamed Pig Street and the King's Arms was known as the Nanny Goat! In 1898, William Walmsley was the landlord at the Kings Arms. This busy man was also a cabinet maker and undertaker. The pub in those days had a bowling alley and was open from 6 in the morning until midnight. Today the Jester serves as both a public house and a restaurant.

Ron Deaville's motor cycle shop at 120, Mill Street occupied the building which was once the Nag's Head. This building replaced another on the same site also called the Nag's Head. George and Mary Spilsbury kept the pub in the 1880s providing both liquid refreshment and excellent meals. The had a large family; some of the children lived in a small house in a court across the road. Today Johnson's Antiques use this property for their business.

The Blue Ball at 129, Mill Street. In the 1960s aspiring rock groups would practice in a room on the first floor where disco's were held. In the 1860s a brewery was attached to the Blue Ball described as "newly erected". In Victorian times the Leek Floral and Horticultural Society held their annual show in this Inn.

The Dyers Arms at 5, Macclesfield Road, another of Leek's old beerhouses, established more than 163 years ago. Originally just one small house, it has been extended over the years, swallowing up property to the side. The row of seven terraced cottages to the right have been demolished and a small one storey extension built on to the Dyers. The rest of the area once occupied by the cottages is used as a car park. Presumably the beer house was so called because of the close proximity of W Hammersley's dye-works at Bridge End and Mill Street. The Dyers Arms is still a very popular establishment and has been kept for several years by Kevin Lewis.

The Conservative Working Mens Club at 210, Mill Street known locally as the "Dog and Rot". The club has existed since 1912 but before that was a drinking establishment called the Spread Eagle. Hezekiah Walmsley was a landlord of the Spread Eagle during the closing years of the 19th Century. Robert Brough was steward of the Conservative Club for many years.

This 18th century building has been used as an inn for a long time. By 1834, it was the Bowling Green Inn and was still known by that name in the 1930s. For some years in the 1960s and 70s it's name changed to the Abbey Green Inn before it reverted back to it's original name. The 'Abbey' as we now know it remains a pleasant venue on the outskirts of Leek. The detached barn reputably constructed from stones taken from Dieulacress Abbey was converted in 1986 to seven luxurious bedrooms for overnight guests.

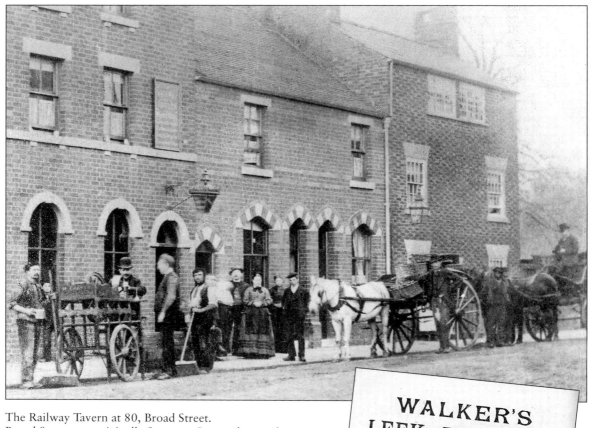

The Railway Tavern at 80, Broad Street.
Broad Street was originally Spooners Lane, afterwards renamed Canal Street. When it was widened to accommodate traffic from the Railway Station, its name was changed to Broad Street. The Railway Tavern obviously provided welcome respite for travellers breaking their journey from the station! From 1898 to at least 1931, the Brentnall family kept the pub. This photograph captures a group of workers outside the tavern. A knife grinder and other tradesman stand outside the pub together with two carts.

George Walker's brewery was situated on the corner of Alsop Street and Canal Street. In 1834 he was one of two brewers in the town and was still in business in 1911. An advertisement of that year reads:

"George Walker , wine and spirit merchant.
27, Broad Street, Leek.
Agent for Whitbreads London Bottled Ales and Stouts.
As supplied to the House of Lords
Guiness Extra Stout
All goods delivered free of charge and carriage paid."

WALKER'S LEEK BREWERY.

Pale, Mild & Bitter Ales and Stout

Absolutely Pure. Always in Condition.
In 4½, 6, 9, 10, 12, or 18 GALLON CASKS,
At Special Low Prices for Cash.

IRISH & SCOTCH WHISKY & RUMS,

From 2/6 per Bottle.

GINS at 2/-, 2/6 and 3/- per Bottle.
BRANDIES from 2/10 " "
WINES " 1/6 " "
All the leading brands of 'Special' Whiskies.

Over 50 years' reputation for purity
and excellence of quality.

☞ ASK FOR PRICE LISTS. ☜

A celebration (below) in the Southbank Hotel (see above also) as Job White's representatives and their wives attend a dinner. Among those pictured are Ken Bowyer and his wife Gladys. In the 1960s the Southbank Hotel advertised that it was AA and RAC approved, had a cocktail bar, garage and central heating. It was open to both residents and non-residents. In 1964 it became The Mulberry Hotel. This year (2001) it has been demolished to make way for new housing.

This photograph was taken in the Central Liberal Club at the time of the 1953 Coronation proving that you can take a horse to water but he would rather have a beer!

The three leopards heads, denoting a fire insurance plaque, can clearly be seen high above the door of the Roebuck. Unfortunately they are no longer with us, presumably having been sold. Whatever the fate of the plaque, an unusual piece of the town's history has now disappeared. A similar plaque on the wall of the house next to the old Co-op shop on Clerk Bank has also now gone.

Two scenes which record the opening of the Park. Councillor James Rhead, Chairman of the Leek Urban District Council, performs the opening ceremony on 21 June 1924.

Above: Park Lodge, part of the Ball Haye estate was once owned by the Brough family who owned Ball Haye Hall.
Below: Brough Park comprises ten and a half acres of ground given to the town by William Spooner Brough from his Ball Haye Estate in 1913, together with a further eight and a half acres given by Joseph Tatton in 1921.
The outbreak of World War I delayed the work on the park, so that it was not officially opened until 1924.
The picturesque grassland and sheltering trees seen here were once part of the Cruso Estate. The Cruso family lived in the house which we now call Foxlowe. Mary Elizabeth Cruso, John Cruso's first wife, spent many happy hours fishing in the pond (see below). The pond has, long since, been filled in. but provided pleasant interludes for Leek lads trying their luck with sticks, string and jam jars.

An early view of a leafy, shady, slumbering Ball Haye Road with the row of large houses on the left called Park Vale. These bay-windowed houses were built by a Mr. Matthews in Edwardian days.

Balle Haye Hall as a private residence.

Lazy days on the bowling green in Brough Park, which was once part of the Ball Haye Estate.

Ball Haye Hall stands as a backdrop to local children engaged in a game of cricket.

Children happily playing around the fountain in the park; a popular local pastime. Unfortunately, the fountain began to be vandalized in later years and the water supply was cut off in 1975. These days the Challinor Fountain proudly stands in the forecourt of Moorlands House in Stockwell Street, where its spouting waters can be seen in operation.

Skating on the frozen duck pond in John Hall's Gardens. A dangerous activity which would be frowned on today. In the early years of the 20th Century local children would earn pennies by putting skates on the feet of people lucky enough to be able to afford them.

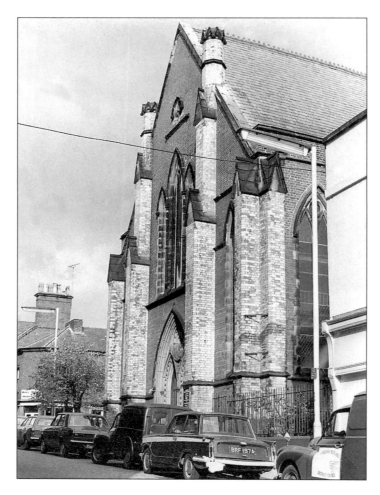

The magnificent gothic-style Brunswick Chapel which stood opposite the Town Hall in Market Street. Built by John Matthews of brick with stone dressings and designed by William Sugden. The cost of building this soaring edifice in 1856 was £4,381. It was the gift of James Wardle. Further improvements were made to the chapel in 1890 at a cost of £1,263.

Regarded as the centre of Methodism in Leek it was found to be structurally unstable resulting in its closure in 1976. Brunswick Chapel was demolished in 1977 and the site of this imposing chapel is now merely a humble car park.

A Primitive Methodist Chapel was built in Fountain Street in 1836 and rebuilt later in 1884. Two hundred and seventeen people attended the Sunday evening service here in 1851. The congregation moved to the New Connection Chapel at the corner of Ball Haye Street and Queen Street in 1949. The old chapel was used for various purposes over the years, once being offices for the Inland Revenue. The former Primitive Methodist Chapel was demolished in the early 1970s. Its location in Fountain Street can be identified by the building on the extreme right of the photograph which is the end of the Cattle Market Inn.

A view looking towards the rear of the chapel.

Fountain Street Methodist Church

LEEK

SUNDAY, 15th DECEMBER, 1946
at 6-0 p.m.

"THE MESSIAH"

(*HANDEL*)

PRINCIPALS :

Soprano : Miss BERYL WOOD
(NEWCASTLE)

Contralto : Miss NELLIE WILLIAMS
(CHESTERTON)

Tenor : Mr. KEITH HOLLINSHEAD
(BADDELEY GREEN)

Bass : Mr. SAM MARTIN
(DURHAM)

Augmented Choir of 75 Voices

Conductor : Mr. PERCY POOLE
Organist : Mr. HARRY G. WHITTER
Presided over by the Rev. HUGH H. BRADLEY

SILVER COLLECTION

Poster for concert at the chapel

In 1856 a society of New Connection Methodists was formed in Leek. Robert Scrivener of Hanley designed this chapel in 1862 for them. It stood at the corner of Queen Street and Ball Haye Street becoming known as Bethesda Chapel by 1875. Ministers of this chapel lived in the two houses attached to the chapel at the bottom of Queen Street. In 1881 at 8, Queen Street lived Thomas Smith a New Connection Minister with his wife Ann and their daughter Jane. They had obviously moved around the country as Thomas was born in Dudley, his wife in Boston, Lincolnshire and their daughter in North Shields, Northumberland.

Although the chapel was closed in the early 1940s it was later used by the Primitive Methodists from Fountain Street. Bethesda Chapel was finally closed in 1963 and after being used for commercial purposes fell into a state of disrepair. The building was demolished in the late 1980s.

These two photographs were taken in Queen Street as the old chapel was being demolished.

The Wesleyan School at the corner of Ball Haye Street and Regent Street was built in 1828. Originally intended to be a Sunday school it was also used for services after James Wardle paid for a gallery and an organ. In 1851, 296 people made up the Sunday evening congregation. Known at first as Brunswick Chapel it was superseded by a chapel of the same name in Market Street. However, the building remained in use as a school until 1914, the pupils transferring to the new County Primary School in East Street. After this date the premises were used for Sunday school classes, church meetings, clinics and as a British Restaurant during World War II. The Leekensians held some of their early productions here and the Magistrates Court operated from here before moving to High Street. In recent years the old schoolrooms and chapel were sold for redevelopment and like its namesake in Market Street, its site is now a car park.

The old schoolrooms lie in ruins as the demolition men move in, 1991.

In 1946, Polish troops from Italy took over the transit camp in Blackshaw Moor which had previously housed American anti-aircraft battalions. Pictured here are Emile and Joseph Swieca who were the first children to arrive at the camp. The Swieca family, along with many of their compatriots, had fled from Poland to Italy before making their way to England.

Polish children taking part in a Corpus Christi ceremony at Blackshaw Moor camp. The large corrugated iron structure behind the children was the camp's church.

Elizabeth Bielecki, Stasia Swieca, Barbara Hryciuk and Danuta Bielecki dressed in traditional costume. The name of the young lady on the extreme left is not known.

More lovely ladies in colourful costumes. Here we see Barbara Hryciuk, Tessie Krzywick, Danuta Hryciuk and Stasia Swieca.

The Polish community was, of course, Roman Catholic and celebrated faithfully the rites, festivals and ceremonies of the church. Here are two photographs of Corpus Christi, which was the festival of the body of Christ.

Thirsty work! One young man's needs are swiftly satisfied as he waits to take part in Leek's traditional Club Day parade. The Polish children were always a captivating and colourful addition to this Summer Sunday School festival.

Walking Round Day (Club Day), passing the Nicholson War Memorial and into Derby Street.

Above left and top right: On Friday 14 August 1914 the 3rd (Leek) Battery, 2nd North Midland Brigade RFA, left the Drill Hall in Alma Street on the first leg of their journey to war. These photographs show the men passing along Belle Vue and out along the Ashbourne Road. Major W F Challinor headed the procession on his horse 'Trumpeter' followed by Lieut. Falkner Nicholson on 'Drake'. Two local policemen walked in front of the battery presumably to clear the way for the horses and to keep back the large crowds who lined the pavements and the roads right up to Lowe Hill Bridge.

Here the Battery with its horse drawn ammunition waggons, guns and soldiers leave Leek by the Ashbourne Road. Jack Blore is riding the lead horse in this photograph. The Battery's first stop was at Waterhouses where refreshments were provided for both horses and men.

In contrast to the cheers and waves of loved ones as they left Leek, stark reality was soon encountered amongst the mud and blood of the trenches. Sidney Simpson M.M., a Leek man, is at the front of the stretcher party on the left. It shows the 15th Field Ambulance in action. It was taken at Chimpai Valley near Montauban on 3rd September 1916. Sid lost a leg in 1918, attending a wounded officer in 'no-man's land'. He died in Dover from gangrene. His body was returned to Leek along with his kit bag which contained his rifle. His younger brother Fred, refused by the Army because of deafness and distraught because of the news of his brother, took the rifle and shot himself at the cemetery gates. His mother buried two sons together, Fred denied a C of E funeral due to his committing suicide. She had three other sons at war, one of whom (Harry) was lost at Arras. Hannah Simpson's experience was no different to thousands of mothers whose plight and anguish is often overlooked today.

Soldiers and sweethearts relax on Rudyard Lake during a brief respite from the horror of war. Sidney Simpson is pictured on the right. He was courting Amy Knight on the far left. After Sid's death, she later married his younger brother, Percy in 1921. The other soldier is Harold Clark.

Civilians, nurses, policemen, St Johns Ambulance men and firemen unite in a Peace Parade after the Great War. The parade is heading down Ashbourne Road as it turns the corner of Parker Street.

Far from the fighting, a young soldier returns to more innocent pastimes as he happily swings with a girlfriend at Pickwood Rec during the 1940s.

A local defence volunteer service was formed in May 1940 and soon received over 600 applications from local men. Although the age limits were 17 to 65, many applications were received from boys under 17, the oldest applicant being 70! Here the assembled ranks of the Leek Home Guard, as they were named, are ready to be inspected by the Earl of Harrowby in October 1940.

Happy smiles on the faces of local Home Guard members as they march in front of the 'Monument'.

On parade. With suitably short hair and forage caps firmly placed, lines of Home Guard members, proceeded by bandsmen, march smartly up Mill Street for a church parade. Crowds of Leek people always gathered to support the local men.

Winston Churchill in typical pose visits the troops during World War II. One of the soldiers pictured here is Winston Harrison, a Leek man.

The Royal Observer Corps – Nan 3 – Rushton Spencer, photographed in 1945.
Back row l-r John Smith Allen, Cope, Allen, N Pale, G Mee and Higginbotham
Front row l-r Smith, Goodfellow, Price, Hulme, Keene and Brown.

VE Day, 1945. Leek people took to the streets, singing, dancing, partying and even climbing lamposts! Above is Sheep Market and below is Livingstone Street, with everyone having a good time.

VE Day, 1945 and Leek youngsters look forward to a bonfire as part of the celebrations. This time it is not Guy Fawkes whom they are going to burn, but an effigy of Hitler.

A little later in the year and residents of Shaw Place gather to celebrate VJ Day.

The Town Hall in Leek is packed with children who are attending a party to celebrate VJ Day. The children all have parents who served as soldiers, sailors or airmen during the war. Mrs HCT Hill had organised the party after money had been collected in local public houses and donations given by Leek residents.

In the early years of the 20th century several junior football clubs existed in Leek. St Lukes, pictured here, was one of the outstanding junior teams, the others being Leek Y.M.C.A., St Mary's, Ball Haye Green and St Edwards. A match between any of these teams was always well attended and worth watching. In 1906 St Lukes was defeated by Y.M.C.A. in the second round of the Combination Cup. Mr TS Myatt had presented this cup in 1893.

Another Leek junior team, this one is Westwood United Football Club in 1908/1909. The young lad in the middle of the front row is Lovatt.

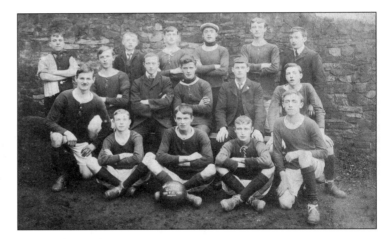

The poster in the window of the Moss Rose indicates that this is the Moss Rose football team. In the late 19th and early 20th centuries football clubs proliferated in the town, factories and public houses having their own teams.

Two photographs of Leek United between the years 1908 to 1911. The second photograph includes P.B. Miller, H. Davenport, John Shallcross, Mr Carding, W.B. Miller, W Rhead, Mr Bowyer, Mr Brough, F Hill and M Riches.

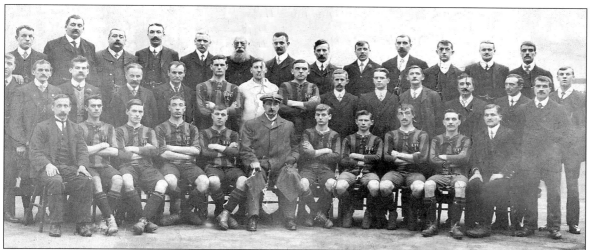

The Cheddleton Mental Hospital team, possibly taken between the Wars. The hospital staff excelled in sporting activities of all kinds. It is rumoured that prospective employees had to have some sporting prowess before gaining employment at Cheddleton!

CHEDDLETON MENTAL HOSPITAL F.C.

Maude Football Club 1924.
Featured are:
Eddie Thonger, Cliff Aggas, Jim
Fisher, Ken Scholes, Edgar Ward,
George Noble, W Walwyn,
H Grindey, H Lockett,
J Hazlehurst and Harry Hall.

Leek Maude Football Club 1925.
In the group are: P Sugden, E
Bennett, Joe Gold, Stan Plant, E
Thonger, George Noble, Cliff
Aggas, W Walwyn, H Mellor,
Claude Allemande, Rev Ernest
Leach, F Allcock, Harold Barlow,
Harold Grindey, Ernie Leese,
George Smith, Jim Fisher, Harry
Hall and Les Fisher.

Wardle's Football Club 1930.
Back row: H Notley, A Moss
(captain), R Rodgers,
G Lyons, L Haywood,
R Dunkley, R Bellington,
S Gosling (Trainer).
Front row: A Johnson, ?
Peacock, G Hambleton, L
Dean, and R Billings.

Leek Scriveners 1936/7
This successful Leek Club
was formed in 1878.

Leek Cricket Club, presumably
at Highfield Hall.
The date is unknown.
W H Goldstraw was held to be
the last underarm bowler for
Leek, but this fact is not
recorded in the History of
Leek Cricket. The club still
plays on the lawn of the
former Hall.

Another group of cricketers.
They appear to be on the
Beggars Lane pitch. in fact it
is Tatton's cricket team
playing in the Leek and
District League in 1954.

Athletic champions in 1953. Proudly holding their trophies and awards are Roy Fowler and Jean Morris with their trainer Fred Smith.

Being put through their paces are Harold Brough, Harry Mace, Roy Fowler, Peter Pointon and Rob White. They were all members of the Parish Church Youth Group who met in the Milward Hall.

The Athletics team from St Edwards Youth Group who took first place in the County Youth Athletic Meeting held in 1953. Included in this photograph are Fred Smith, Hazel Fowler, the Leith twins, Alan Robinson, John Moreton, Peter Lowe, Harry Mace, John Mellor, Stuart Raine, Harry Higginbotham, Marian Hilditch, Roy Fowler and Jean Morris.

A trip on a charabanc was always a pleasant pastime enjoyed by the people of Leek.
Here two different vehicles packed with passengers are ready to begin their journeys to the countryside or the coast. Mr Thomas Porter's charabanc in Bath Street stands outside his premises, a board advertising trips to Buxton for 2/6d can be clearly seen. The other vehicle is parked outside the Park Tavern in Ball Haye Road and is obviously a 'men only' occasion.

A selection of carnival floats made by W Turner and Sons, builders of Leek. Much ingenuity and imagination went into the design of these floats which quite often won prizes. In the 1920s and 30s the carnival procession made slow progress with frequent stops. The men on the floats provided entertainment for the crowds, at these times, by jumping off the floats carrying a paper stretcher and loading a 'patient' on to it. He would promptly fall through the paper to the amusement of the crowd!

1st Leek Guides at the 1982 Carnival.
The dormouse is Jean Parr; front row far left is Carol Heath, then Emma Brooks, with the cup is Vanessa Beech, the White Rabbit is Kerry Peacock and the Mad Hatter is Kay Hiscock. Tweedle Dum/ Dee were Louise Beeby (left) and Rachel Binns (right).

St Edwards Youth Drama Society performing at the Milward Hall. The actors include Sheila Fallon, Ian Coghill and Elizabeth Gildart.

Leek Amateur Dramatic Society present 'Bonaventure' at Leek Town Hall.
Pictured here are Kathleen West, Ian Coghill, June Potts, Andre Bold, Freda Davies, Nella and Dorothy Parker, Sheila Fallon, Gwen Nicholson and Charles Brown.

Leek and District Youth Clubs netball team c 1960. Kneeling are Dorothy Nettel, Diane Clarke, Bernice Hall and Marian Binns.

Children from Compton School on a class visit to Pickwood Rec. Standing patiently in the line they wait to climb the ladder in order to whizz down the slippery slope of the shute. Two of the children in the photograph are Anita Willman and Alan Vigrass.

Gypsy Girls at the 1960 Ball Haye Green Carnival. The 3rd Leek Guides here are l-r: Hazel Vernon, Joan Pointon, Pat Rowlinson, Caroline Mellor, Anne Wright, Vickie Poyser and Yvonne Porter.

Partytime in the canteen of Adams Butter at Springfield Road.

A Christmas party at the Co-op Hall in Ashbourne Road in c.1962.

Proud mums and blissful babies abound in this Christmas photograph taken in the Sadler Ward at Leek Hospital.

Dr Sadler at the Moorlands Hospital with Sister Lancaster with Percy Walton and Dr Cox (2nd from right).

This is probably a meeting of the Mothers Union of All Saints Church in the 1950s

Taken c. 1960, this is the Leek Bowling Club dinner. Featured are Arthur Goldstraw, (top left hand corner) and his father Henry and brother Stanley (front row, 2nd and 4th from left). All three used to play together in the first team and in 1947, they were joined, for the first time, in a match at Cheadle, by Stanley's son Norman. It was a proud event for the family.

Miss Elsie Lowe, the 1938 Textile Queen, can be seen in the centre of this photograph. A concert entitled 'The Musical Box' was held at the New Grand Theatre in 1938 to raise money for the Leek Carnival and Charities Committee. Who can recognise Ray Morrow, Frank Nadin, Norman Pickford, Ken Bowyer, Charles Kunz and Harold Wardle amongst others. The money raised at this event was meant for the fund set up to convert Ball Haye Hall into a hospital. Leek people were disappointed and angry when this didn't happen.

10th Leek (Brunswick) Scouts parade down Brook Street with leader Norman Morris on Club Day, ahead of the Brunswick Methodist Sunday School banner. The houses to the left of the parade have all been demolished.

Drummers from 1st Leek Scouts in 1958, near to the Coffee Tavern.

1st Leek cubs in 1954

About to board a van in Belle Vue are members of 1st Leek Scout Group. They were off to Switzerland, some in the standard uniform, complete with long shorts and others less conventionally attired.

Scouts and cubs of 4th Leek await their order to move on Club Day in the early 1960s. They are gathered on the Red Lion Yard area.

The parade marking the centenary of the Nicholson Institute passes along the bottom of Derby Street in 1984. Clive Joynson, the Leek librarian, steps out smartly, followed by Jim and Pauline Clowes. Pauline wrote the history of the Nicholson Institute.

The Remembrance Parade of November 1998. Old soldiers, young air cadets and members of the St John's Ambulance Brigade gather together in homage around the Nicholson War Memorial.

Familiar faces from the indoor market stalls as stallholders don Victorian garb to celebrate the centenary of the Butter Market.

Below: the British Legion band in May 1932; winners of the Besson Challenge Cup. Back Row (l-r): F Morley, C Goodwin, H Johnson, B Trafford; 2nd Row: W Beresford, J Guilford, A Sheldon, G Fowell, Bert Harper; 3rd Row: W Fowler, S Fitch, R Martin Snr, F Birch, G Spooner, G Edge, H Hammond, R Birch, A Birch; Front Row: A Murfin, J Putnam, T Hambleton, H Mortimer, G Worthington, W Carter, A Hawse, R Martin Jnr, F Wright.

It's the 25th May 1990 as this magnificent monk flanked by two buxom wenches takes part in the Pied Poudre celebrations in Derby Street.

Linda Malyon, Lindsey Porter, Cathryn Walton and John Fisher at the launch of 'Spirit of Leek, Volume 1' and 'Staffordshire Moorlands and the Churnet Valley'. This successful launch was held at The Swan in St Edward Street.